"Love and compassion
are necessities, not luxuries.
Without them humanity
cannot survive."

His Holiness the Dalai Lama

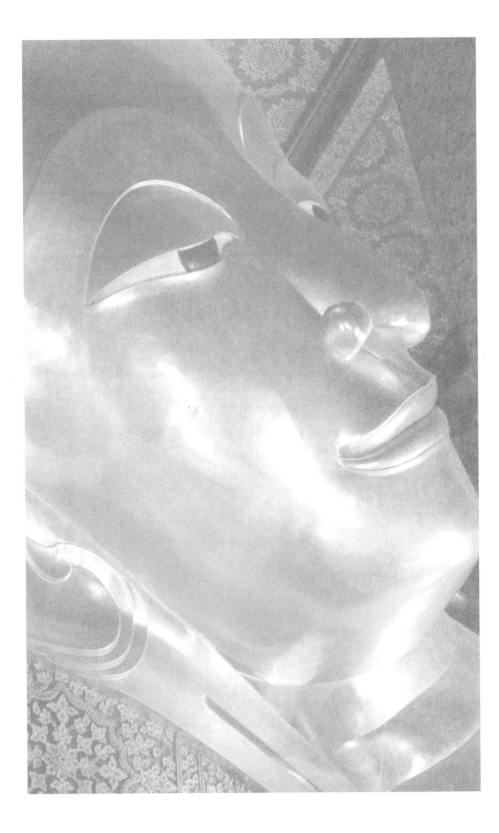

a year of
Living
with more
Compassion

52
Quotes & Weekly Compassion Practices

Richard Fields, PhD – Editor

Published by FACES Conferences
Tucson, AZ
www.facesconferences.com

This book is dedicated to my wonderful

mother, Libby Fields

A note of gratitude to all our FACES Conferences (facesconferences.com)
master teachers who contributed to our book.

Thanks to Jack Kornfield and Tara Brach for embracing
the mission of this book and for their support.

A special thanks to Chris Germer and Kristin Neff for their inspiration,
suggestions, and commitment to making this book a reality.

Thanks to Monique Kornell for her timely and thorough editing of the book
and to Audrey Hall (www.audreyhalldesign.com) for designing the cover.

Of course, our gratitude to our talented designer
Don Stayner (www.dsdwerx.com), whose commitment to this project
is so elegantly reflected in these pages.

 *Table of Contents*

SECTION VIII ▪ *Compassion, Hate, & Difficult People*
QUOTES NO. 40–42

SECTION IX ▪ *Compassion for Challenging Situations*
QUOTES NO. 43–52

APPENDIX

More Compassion In Your Life

This handbook of compassion quotes, lessons, and practices is designed to help you increase your capacity for self-compassion and compassion for others. The book is a way for our extraordinary teachers, who present at FACES Conferences (www.facesconferences.com), to bring compassion skills to your life.

The Method

Each of the thirty-six of our FACES Conferences master teachers from the fields of psychology, mindfulness, and compassion selected his or her favorite compassion quote, explained the compassion lesson for that quote, and included a compassion practice for the week. The quote, the lesson, and the compassion practice all will help you, the reader, open up to and develop more compassion in your life.

Our Teachers

I express my gratitude to our wonderful master teachers, leaders in their fields, innovators, researchers, clinicians/therapists, many of whom are devoted to special projects for people in need. Our teachers are remarkably gifted and talented people with good hearts.

How To Use This Book

This book is designed to help you focus on one compassion quote and practice per week. It is suggested that you display the quote for the week on your computer, or on your cell phone, or even on your kitchen refrigerator (always a good place to remember to be self-compassionate). You might also choose to memorize the quote or compassion theme of the week, or keep it in your consciousness. Try adopting the mantra of "compassion", "self-compassion", or "kindness", repeating that to yourself to help you focus on being more compassionate.

You can then follow the compassion practice for that week for that quote. It is also suggested that during each week you keep a journal. One or more times a week write down any observations, awareness, attentions, feelings, and intentions that might arise.

Why 52 Quotes?

We have 52 Quotes so you have one quote to work with for each week of the year. The Buddha habitually numbered things – the 4 noble truths, the 8-fold path. In that tradition we chose 52 Quotes for our format.

Quote Sections

The quotes we received from our master teachers, while all independent of each other, touch on several overlapping themes. They are organized into nine sections.

Section I – *Heart & Love*

Section II – *Opening to Compassion: Overcoming "Compassion Resistance"*

Section III – *Kindness*

Section IV – *Self-Compassion*

Section V – *Interconnectedness*

Section VI – *Compassion & the Body*

Section VII – *Important Aspects of Compassion*

Section VIII – *Compassion, Hate, & Difficult People*

Section IX – *Compassion for Difficult & Challenging Situations*

Guidelines

You might notice that you have favorite quotes, love and enjoy certain quotes and find their associated compassion practices engaging and uplifting. You will also find that certain compassion quotes and practices cause discomfort and difficult emotions. These quotes may lead to new and valuable insights that would benefit from further exploration. We encourage you to practice self-compassion, giving yourself time to process some of the issues or feelings that might arise. Remember the goal of the book is to increase compassion in your life. If you find that negative emotions are blocking you from experiencing more self-compassion, and compassion for others, you might seek counsel from a therapist/counselor, teacher, coach, or spiritual guide to help unblock what is holding you back or causing resistance.

These are just guidelines for using the book. Feel free to use the book as you see fit. Maybe you will skim through the book picking the quote and practice on which you want to focus. Some people will even randomly flip through the book and pick a quote and practice. It also is a good idea to read a few quotes or a section, especially when you feel your self-compassion and compassion fuel tank is running low. It is up to you.

The hope and mission of this book is to help you achieve more self-compassion and compassion in your life. The shift to more self-compassion is an important one that counters the self-blame, self-loathing, self-critical, and self-limiting parts of you that you do not like. This book will help you increase your capacity for self-compassion and compassion for others, leading towards a healthier and more fulfilling life.

Why Compassion is Important

Compassion is nothing new. It has a long and noble history. It's at the core of all the world's religions and hardwired into our DNA. Confucius said, "Never do to others what you would not like them to do to you." Charles Darwin observed that "those communities, which included the greatest number of the most sympathetic members, would flourish best."

Over the last few years, there has been a burgeoning scientific interest in compassion that is changing our understanding of it. There is new recognition that compassion is good for you – *very* good for you, being closely related to happiness, wisdom, emotional resilience, better relationships, improved health, and a host of other factors.

Compassion is a *strength* that allows us to transform emotional suffering, it is a *skill* that can be learned, and it can be *directed toward oneself.* Brain scans are demonstrating that compassion activates pleasure centers even in the presence of suffering, transforming pain for the better. But a warmhearted response to suffering may not automatically arise in us, especially when we feel frightened by it. Compassion training can help us develop the skill of compassion through deliberate mental practice, changing the brain for the better even after only a few weeks of practicing methods such as those described in this book. Finally, our new, scientifically-informed model of compassion indicates that we can give compassion to ourselves when we need it the most. Cultivating a warm, connected presence with ourselves provides a basis for our capacity to be compassionate to others.

The current interest in compassion seems to be the next step in the unprecedented convergence of ancient Buddhist psychology and practice with modern scientific psychology. The first step was mindfulness, which may be considered the foundation of compassion. Our emerging reinterpretation of compassion is starting to transform, albeit still in small ways, how we approach mental health, education, parenting, and areas of our professional life. It's becoming a new meme – a transmittable cultural idea. This change cannot come soon enough, however, if we reflect even for a moment on the complex challenges facing humanity today.

The 52 quotes in this book, their interpretations, and the compassion practices are a beautiful blend of the old and the new. Many of the contributors are currently evolving our modern understanding of compassion and they share here some of their own inspirations. They also offer simple, yet profound suggestions for actualizing the benefits of compassion in our own lives. **If you allow this book to be a bedside companion for the next year, your life may never be the same.**

Christopher Germer, PhD
Coeditor, Wisdom and Compassion in Psychotherapy, *2012*

Heart & Love

JACK KORNFIELD, PhD, chose this quote:

66

I am larger and better than I thought. I did not think I held so much goodness.

99

Walt Whitman

THEME – *Compassion & the Heart*

"Oh, nobly born, remember your own loving heart. Trust it, honor it, follow it. It will bring you peace." – *The Buddha*

The human heart has the extraordinary capacity to transform the sorrows of life into a great stream of compassion. Compassion proclaims the power of the tender and merciful heart in the face of the suffering of the world. It arises whenever we allow our hearts to be touched by the pain and need of another.

COMPASSION PRACTICE

To cultivate compassion, let yourself sit in a centered and quiet way. Breathe softly and feel your body, your heartbeat, and the life within you. Feel how you treasure your own life, how you guard yourself in the face of your sorrow.

After some time, bring to mind someone close to you whom you dearly love. Picture them and feel your natural caring for them. Notice how you hold them in your heart.

Then let yourself be aware of their sorrows, their measure of suffering in life. Feel how your heart opens to wish them well; to extend comfort to them; to share in their pain and meet them with compassion.

To open your heart still further, begin reciting the phrases:
__"May you be held in compassion.__
__May your pain and sorrows be eased.__
__May you be at peace."__

Continue reciting the phrases while you are holding them in your heart.

After you feel your deep caring for this person close to you, turn the same compassionate heart toward yourself.

Place your hands over your own heart, while you recite:
__"May I be held in compassion,__
__May my pain and sorrow be eased.__
__May I be at peace."__

Now, one person at a time, extend your compassion to others you know. Picture loved ones, one after another. Hold the image of each in your heart, be aware of their difficulties and wish them well, as you recite:
__"May you be held in compassion.__
__May your pain and sorrow be eased.__
__May you be at peace."__

Now you can open your compassion further to the suffering of your friends, to your neighbors, your community, to all who suffer, to difficult people, to your enemies, and finally to the brotherhood and sisterhood of all beings.

2

"

Admit something:
Everyone you see, you say to them,
'Love me.' Of course you do not do this
out loud, otherwise someone would
call the cops. Still, though, think about
this, this great pull in us to connect.
Why not become the one who lives
with a full moon in each eye that is
always saying, with that sweet moon
language, what every other eye in this
world is dying to hear?

"

Hafiz, With That Moon Language, in
The Gift: Poems by Hafiz, the great Sufi Master,
D. Ladinsky, trans., 1999

THEME – *The Desire & Drive to Be Loved & to Love*

These words come to us from the 14th century, but they could easily have been written today. **The pull to connect is a deep urge or drive within all human beings**, as it is in most mammals that have learned to survive by connecting with one another.

If newborn babies could speak, their first words might sound a lot like "Love me!" Fortunately, babies are good at getting adults to love them and whatever they need naturally follows.

Do we ever stop saying, "Love me" just because our bodies have aged? I doubt it. Like children, we look for signs of warmth and friendliness in the eyes of almost everyone we meet and we feel subtly wounded if a whole day passes without receiving any affection. A host of good feelings arise when we feel loved, such as joy, gratitude, generosity, and hope. Similarly, the pain of disconnection from others is associated with negative emotions such as anger, fear, and shame.

Curiously, we tend to forget the wise words of Hafiz and live our lives as if it doesn't matter whether we're loved, spending much of our lives in pursuit of material possessions and using people to achieve our personal goals rather than valuing warmth and connection. Perhaps the pain of disconnection has made us stop caring. But what would happen if we woke up every morning consciously aware that, like all human beings, we wish to be loved? The root of compassion is intimate contact with suffering. How about the universal hunger to be seen, heard, touched, and known? When our hearts are open to this yearning, we seem to discover the same in others and respond in kind.

The opposite reaction is sadly familiar. When we forget that everyone wishes to be loved and when the pain of disconnection arrives at our door, our feelings become hard, often with anger and resentment. But **when we peel back the onion of anger, we find softer emotions lying underneath, such as fear, loneliness, or confusion.** And still deeper, we discover the unmet need to be loved and connected. Lingering in awareness with this underlying need can protect us from a lot of unnecessary anguish.

To love and be loved is part of your deepest nature and is more essential than whatever or whoever you think you are.

When we see how this "great pull in us to connect" motivates much of what we think and do, then the mind becomes quiet, the heart opens, and we begin to see others with new, more compassionate eyes.

COMPASSION PRACTICE

Before you get out of bed in the morning, put your hands over your heart and remind yourself, "I, and all beings, wish to be loved."

3

RICHARD C. SCHWARTZ, PhD, chose this quote:

"

Then it was as if I suddenly saw the secret beauty of their hearts, the depth of their hearts where neither sin nor desire nor self-knowledge can reach, the core of their reality, the person that each one is in the eyes of the Divine. If only they could all see themselves as they really are. If only we could see each other that way all the time. There would be no more war, no more hatred, no more greed... I suppose the big problem would be that we would fall down and worship each other.

"

Thomas Merton

THEME – *The Secret Beauty of The Heart*

If you have had an experience like the one Merton describes, it is unforgettable, but also fleeting. **There are protective parts of all of us that maintain the optical delusion of separateness.** They limit our ability to see the divine beauty in others, and, relatedly, keep our circle of compassion small so we are not overwhelmed by the pain in the world and don't spend all our time trying to change it.

Fortunately, however, there is a place within us where we know we are connected to the sacred in each other and, consequently, from that place we have an enormous circle of compassion. I call this inner essence the Self and find that it is just behind the walls erected by our inner protectors. This means that we don't have to meditate twenty years before we can attain it. Instead this calm, compassionate Self will emerge spontaneously once the parts of us that occlude it trust that it is safe to relax and open space inside.

COMPASSION PRACTICE

No matter how hard we work to be openhearted we all have parts of us (sometimes unconscious) that give us negative or fearful thoughts and emotions regarding a person we consider different or dangerous.

Think of such a person in your life that you fear or disdain, or a group of people that, at some level, you fear or disdain, and then imagine a single person from that group. Notice how you feel toward this person as you consider him or her. Now, pretend that you have x-ray vision and can see inside that person. As you look inside, notice that the protective parts of that person that scare you or that you don't like are protecting their hurt and vulnerable parts.

Then notice that, deep within them, behind both the protection and vulnerability, is a radiant, pulsating light. Stay focused on that light until you start to feel it in yourself, beneath your own protective parts. Look again at the person and see how you feel toward him or her now.

BROOKE DODSON-LAVELLE, MA, chose this quote:

66

It felt love.
How did the rose ever
open its heart and give to
this world all its beauty?
It felt the encouragement
of light against its being,
otherwise, we all remain
too frightened.

99

Hafiz

THEME – *The Capacity for Love*

Learning to open to others and love more deeply requires profound courage and vulnerability. So often we are held back by fear – fear of loss, disconnection, unworthiness, or even further trauma – that we are unable to fully give ourselves over to love.

Giving love requires that we first feel and receive love. As we learn to recognize and connect more deeply to the sources of love that are all around us, we are empowered to open our hearts more and more fully to others. We can learn to sense the light that is all around us, continually encouraging us, by tuning in to the moments in our lives when we felt seen, loved, and accepted by another. These can be moments in which we felt heard, acknowledged, or completely at ease. These can also be moments in which we felt recognized in our fuller being.

Recalling these moments of deep connection that we have experienced in the presence of another person, mentor, or even spiritual teacher helps us tune into the profound well of love and beauty that is within and around each of us. With practice, we begin to recognize our limitless capacity for love and come to be healed by it as we slowly and tenderly drive out the fear that has restrained our hearts. **As we learn to lean in to and abide in the light that is love, we invite the beauty of our hearts to flow forth, blessing others in its wake.**

COMPASSION PRACTICE

*The following practice is adapted from the teachings
of one of my mentors, John Makransky.*

*Sit in a relaxed way, and try to bring to mind
one or more "benefactor moments" – moments when you
felt seen, deeply accepted and loved. These moments can be
times in which someone dear to you or even a stranger
extended the wish of love to you, perhaps through a
gentle smile, kind gesture, or a welcoming presence.*

*Imagine that moment is present now, and notice
the happiness of holding that benefactor in mind. Be at ease,
gently allowing yourself to open, allow, and accept their wish
of love for you to whatever extent you can right now. Relax into
and allow this love to infuse every part of your body and mind.*

*After a few moments, release the visualization and allow
yourself to simply let go into that joyful feeling of love and
acceptance. Take a moment to enjoy being at ease and complete.*

5

The door to the human heart can be opened only from the inside.

Spanish Proverb

THEME – *The Compassionate Heart Center*

Even the greatest of poets cannot describe the depth of compassion and love that the human heart can experience. **In spiritual practice, we refer to the "heart center" rather than the heart as an organ.** It can be an indicator of what is going on within us. We're so inundated with "get out there and do it" messages that the energy spent just being with another person can appear to be doing nothing at all. Yet, connecting heart to heart is anything *but* doing nothing. Being in touch with our heart center and making genuine heart-to-heart contact with another requires energy and attentiveness. How do we start? What can we do in our busy lives to be more in touch with our own heart center? We could start by stopping – stopping to take a moment in stillness. We could enjoy a long gentle in-breath and a long outward sigh. (How about right now?) We could lighten up – even a little bit can help. **A heart can become heavy both spiritually and physiologically, especially when its companion is a relentless mind.** We could walk on the earth (even if it's paved over with concrete), smell a flower, sing a song, dance with a friend, and offer a smile to that person in the mirror.

Our greatest happiness comes from the experience of love and compassion. The more we genuinely care about others, the greater our own happiness and inner peace. So, loving others is the greatest gift we can give ourselves. It's almost a contradiction – altruism that rewards one's self. For each of us, there are those we find easier to love and those we find more challenging. But the practice of being a loving, compassionate person allows no boundaries; no one can be excluded. Those who push our buttons – who appear rude, arrogant, greedy – these are the very people with whom we can refine our practice. No matter how different the look, behavior, customs, or costumes, there is no significant difference among people. A loving, compassionate person recognizes that our basic natures are the same. We all want to be happy and we all want to be loved.

COMPASSION PRACTICE

Each day, offer thoughts of loving kindness to
yourself and to all beings.

Think gently to yourself:
May all beings be safe.
May all beings be happy.
May all beings be healthy.
May all beings live with ease.
May all beings live in peace.
May my life be of benefit to all beings.

To "live with ease" refers to dealing with our everyday activities –
home life, the workplace, the kids, traffic, and so forth –
free from stress and turmoil.

*If you are going through a difficult period,
or if it just feels right, it's fine to focus
primarily on yourself: May I be safe, may I be happy, etc.*

*If you know of someone who is going through a
particularly difficult time, you might want to focus
primarily on him or her. Envision them and think:
May you be safe, may you be happy, etc. It's nice to end by
offering* metta *to all beings: May all beings be safe, etc.
Feel free to alter the wording so that it feels right for you.
Offer the thoughts at a pace that enables you to
maintain concentration from one sentence to the next.*

Opening to Compassion: Overcoming "Compassion Resistance"

6

TARA BRACH, PhD, chose this quote:

"

Could a greater miracle take place than for us to look through each other's eyes for an instant?

"

Henry David Thoreau, Walden, *1854, in*
The Writings of Henry David Thoreau, *vol. 2, 1906, p. 11*

THEME – Tonglen: *Awakening the Heart of Compassion by Unlocking the Armor of Our Heart*

The capacity for compassion is hardwired into our brain and body. Just as we are rigged to perceive differences, to feel separate, and to react with aversion, we are also designed to feel a connection with our fellow humans. Specialized "mirror neurons" attune us to another person's state – to their emotions and the intentions behind their movements – and recreate that state in our own brain. Our experience of them is not just a projection based on visible expressions like grimaces, narrowed eyes, or furrowed brows. Because of mirror neurons, and other structures in the prefrontal cortex that make up our compassion circuitry, we can actually "feel with" them.

Yet these compassion circuits are easily blocked when we're stressed and out of touch with our emotions and bodies. They can also become blocked when we're experiencing unexamined reactivity to the people in our life. Research shows that the less we identify with someone – the less they seem real to us – the less the mirror neuron system gets activated.

The good news is that we can unblock and activate our compassion networks. When we mindfully recognize that another is hurt or afraid, we naturally feel the tenderness of compassion. That tenderness blossoms fully as we find ways to express our care. This alchemy of letting ourselves be touched by another's pain and of responding with love is the essence of Buddhist compassion practices.

One such meditation, the Tibetan practice of *tonglen*, directly awakens our capacity for seeing through another's eyes and offering care. **The starting place in *tonglen* is an intentional relaxing of the armoring around our heart.** Each of us has been wounded, and in reaction, has erected defenses to protect ourselves from experiencing further harm. We don't want to be vulnerable or available to pain. Yet before we can be tenderhearted, we have to be tender. As poet Mark Nepo writes:

"Our challenge each day is not to get dressed to face the world, but to unglove ourselves so that the doorknob feels cold, and the car handle feels wet, and the kiss goodbye feels like the lips of another being, soft and unrepeatable."

Compassion – for ourselves, each other, and all living beings – is an innate part of our evolutionary potential. While we have strong conditioning to close down, we also aspire to awaken our hearts and realize our belonging to each other. This longing is the compass of our heart; it is our guide to happiness, freedom, and the healing of our world.

Tonglen: *Awakening the Heart of Compassion*

Sit in a way that allows you to be relaxed and alert. Let go of any habitual tension and allow your body and mind to settle.

The traditional practice of tonglen *begins by taking a moment to sense the stillness or openness that is already here. This is considered a flash of remembrance, a reconnecting with our awakened heart and mind.*

Now bring your attention to the natural rhythm and quality of your breath. As the breath flows in, allow your cells to receive this life energy. With each in breath, open with total receptivity, like a balloon gently expanding with air. Be aware of the experience of no resistance, of allowing yourself to be touched by the sensations of the breath.

With the out- breath, notice the sensations of letting go and releasing into the space that surrounds you. Imagine your total body and consciousness flowing outward with the breath and mingling with the vastness of space. Breathe out into relaxation, ease, and spaciousness.

Continue meditating on the essence of receiving, being touched with the in- breath, and letting go into openness with the out- breath.

Now invite into your awareness someone you know personally who is suffering, someone you want to help. Imagine yourself in this person's circumstances, experiencing this person's fear or hurt or loss. What is it like to look at the world through these eyes? Live inside this particular body? Feel with this heart? What is the most vulnerable, painful part of this person's experience? What does he or she most need?

Now breathing in, invite all this pain into your heart, allowing yourself to feel it fully. Breathe in, taking the pain into yourself, so that the other person will have relief.

And as you breathe out, respond to his or her needs by sending out relaxation, space, love, or whatever will bring ease and happiness.

Sometimes as you breathe in, you will meet your own resistance to pain. If this happens, shift the focus and breathe for yourself and countless others just like you who are feeling this same frustration, anger, revulsion, or fear. Then as you breathe out, offer whatever helps you and others like you find space and relief.

As your resistance softens, return to breathing for the person you intend to help. As you inhale and let the person's pain touch you, feel how he or she is held in your heart. And as you exhale, send whatever prayer or expression of care feels most sincere or most needed.

Now, enlarge the taking in and sending out to include all those who are in the same situation, experiencing the same suffering. If the person you want to help is grieving a loss, breathe in and out for all those who are experiencing the pain of loss. If this person feels like a failure, breathe in and out for all who feel like failures. Sense, as you breathe in, the unconditional willingness, tenderness, and receptivity of your heart; and as you breathe out, the vastness of loving awareness that is here, holding this world.

Continue breathing, opening to the universal experience of this suffering and letting go into spaciousness with prayer. As your heart opens to the enormity of suffering, you become that openness. As you offer your tenderness, your awareness becomes suffused with compassion.

Flexibility in using the breath: If at any point you find the breathing instructions interfere with the actual experience of taking in suffering and sending out ease and love, adjust to however it most serves the meditation. For instance, you might find you need to focus on just the in- breath or just the out- breath for several cycles to more fully contact experience, or to let go. Or you might find that it is easier not to focus on the breath at all.

Throughout your day: You can do an abbreviated version of tonglen *whenever you encounter suffering. If someone you meet is having a hard time, pause. For several breaths, silently breathe in his or her pain and breathe out relief. If you feel yourself resisting, turned off, or afraid of the pain, do* tonglen *for yourself and all those like you who are having difficulty opening to pain.*

No matter what comes up, it is an opportunity for practicing compassion. Rather than ignoring pain or judging ourselves, we can train ourselves to open into our full potential to love.

Note: Tonglen *may be inappropriate if you are struggling with trauma-related fear, unrelenting depression, or severe psychological imbalance.* Tonglen *may then cause emotional flooding or a sense of being stuck. In these situations, seek guidance from a spiritual teacher, therapist, or trusted guide in finding what best helps you move toward healing.*

7

RICHARD C. SCHWARTZ, PhD, chose this quote:

66

Your task is not to seek for love, but merely to seek and find all the barriers within yourself that you have built against it.

99

Rumi (1207-1273)

THEME – *Releasing Your Love & Compassion*

Rumi's advice is sage because it implies that the problem isn't that we need to develop the capacity for love and compassion; instead, it already exists within us and our task is to release what is already there, like the sun behind the clouds. To do that he asks us to find the clouds we have built against that inner light. But, if such wonderful capacities already exist inside, why would we build barriers to this essence?

Opening one's heart involves risking being vulnerable. When we remain narcissistically insulated, fearfully isolated, driven to distractions or to alcohol/ drugs, we can avoid the adventures of the heart that have gotten us hurt in the past. Most of us have protective parts that share Bilbo Baggins' approach to life that he advocated in the Hobbit, "We're just plain quiet folk and have no use for adventures. Nasty disturbing uncomfortable things. Make you late for dinner. I can't think what anybody sees in them."

Suppose we take Rumi's advice and find these protective parts in us, how do we convince them to drop their weapons when it is true that the risks of vulnerability are extremely high? If we care about people, they in turn could abandon, humiliate, or control us. If we weren't so self-involved, we could wind up re-experiencing shame, rejection, anxiety, or other nasty, disturbing, uncomfortable things. Why take such risks?

The answer is that we have to lower the risk in order to achieve more of what Brené Brown calls "shame resilience." It turns out that those uncomfortable feelings are contained by young, vulnerable parts of us that are frozen in past times when we were hurt or shamed and whenever anything similar happens in the present, all those feelings are reactivated and overwhelm us. Once we heal those hurting parts, then vulnerability isn't so scary, the stakes are lower and our protective parts will step down, allowing our inner sun to shine on those around us and on those who suffer around the world. In addition, with that healing, we won't have to spend so much time and energy trying to fill the emptiness or compensate for the worthlessness inside with the accolades of others or with material things, because we will have a stronger sense of our own inherent worth. There becomes more space in our sphere of compassion when it isn't so cluttered by our frantic striving.

Think of a person to whom have closed your heart.
This could be a family member, intimate partner, colleague,
anyone you choose. Then, in your imagination, put that person
in a room by him or herself, such that you are looking at him
or her from outside the room through a window.

Now focus on the state of your heart in your chest and notice
where it feels closed, calloused, crusted, or congested.
Focus on one of those protective feelings and try to open your mind
to the part of you that is keeping your heart that way. Ask that feeling
what it is afraid would happen if it didn't protect your heart that
way and wait for an answer to come, rather than trying to think
of the answer. That answer will likely give you a hint regarding
the hurt part that it protects, so see if you can show the protector
appreciation for trying to protect you that way, and ask if it would
be willing to let you get to know more about the hurt part it protects.
If the answer is "no," respect that answer and find a therapist
to help you with the next steps. If the answer is "yes," ask the
hurt part to tell you about itself and why it is so hurt. As it does so,
see if you can show it compassion; in other words you are extending
love to a younger version of yourself.

Simply compassionately witnessing the pain of this hurt part of you
will go a long way toward healing it and making you less vulnerable to the
person in the room. Then it will be safer to open your heart to him or her.

8

ALLAN LOKOS chose this quote:

66

One of the effects of fear is to disturb the senses and cause things to appear to be other than what they are.

99

Miguel de Cervantes, Don Quixote, *1607-15*

THEME – *Fear & Compassion*

I believe that the opposite of love and compassion is fear. Fear is an obstacle to love. Fear is an opponent of compassion, and a formidable opponent at that. Wisdom is seeing things as they really are. Therefore, it would follow that developing a kind and loving heart would help us live more wisely. A useful rule to remember is: **if it looks like wisdom, but is unkind, it is not wisdom; if it feels like compassion, but is not wise, it is not compassion.** Significantly, love and fear cannot be active in us at the same time. In other words, if we are thinking, speaking, and acting from a truly loving place within, we are not experiencing fear. Conversely, **if our thoughts, words, or deeds are motivated by fear, we will not be acting with compassion.** At such moments, we might think that if so-and-so didn't act that way, or if such-and-such hadn't happened, we would be happier, which might be so. But circumstances and conditions are as they are, and it is how we experience them that determine our happiness. Louisa May Alcott apparently understood this when she said, **"I'm not afraid of storms, for I'm learning to sail my ship."**

What most of us want is to be accepted unconditionally for who we are, with our mistakes and unskillfulness. Likewise, we need to accept others for who they are. We need to realize that the wishes, desires, and needs of others are as important to them as ours are to us. To be a loving, compassionate person is to understand that we are all fellow travelers on this journey, that we all experience the joys and sorrows that comprise this adventure called life.

The practice of *metta*, or loving kindness, as taught in the Buddhist tradition, is the offering of loving thoughts first to one's self and then, progressively, to all beings. This practice of offering thoughts of loving kindness can dissolve fear, anger, and greed, which are the saboteurs of love. The ultimate *metta* practice is to become a loving person in even the most challenging and abusive situations. This does not mean becoming a doormat, but rather being one who acts with compassion in any circumstance. **In some of us the seed of love may have gone dormant because it has not received the light, warmth, and nutrients needed for its growth. But love is like the sun: no matter how many cloudy days hide its face it is always there, ready to shine through in the next moment.**

COMPASSION PRACTICE

When feeling angry, tense, or anxious, remind yourself that these feelings are grounded in fear. Stop and try to identify the cause of the fear.

When you experience impatience, resentment, or anger, stop and ask yourself, "All right, what is this fear?" It can be difficult for some of us to acknowledge fear, but it is an absolutely normal feeling and part of the human condition. Ask yourself again quietly, "What is this fear?" Remember, thoughts, words, emotions, and deeds not coming from love and compassion are likely coming from fear.

9

C. DARYL CAMERON, PhD, chose this quote:

❝

If I look at the mass, I will never act. If I look at the one, I will.

❞

Mother Teresa

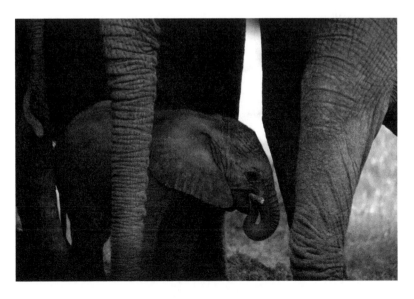

THEME – *Expanding Instead of Collapsing Compassion*

This quote speaks to a situation that many of us face when others are suffering: being afraid that compassion will be overwhelming. Because of these fears, many people choose to avoid their compassion for others. These fears of compassion can be resolved, however, by learning more about the science of compassion.

We often read about natural disasters, genocides, and other large-scale tragedies where many lives are lost or at stake. Given the value of each life, we predict that we would – and *should* – feel more compassion for many victims than for a single victim. Yet many studies show exactly the opposite; we feel more compassion for one victim than for many victims. **Compassion collapses as the numbers increase, precisely when we need to feel it the most.**

Some scholars have suggested that compassion is a limited resource, that we simply cannot feel compassion when a lot of people are involved in a crisis. This claim has led to a suggestion that compassion is not a trustworthy guide for moral behavior. My research suggests a very different story, that **we are afraid of letting ourselves feel compassion for many victims.** Because of these fears, we strategically eliminate our compassion to avoid its costs. **The collapse of compassion between one and many victims only emerges when people are motivated to avoid compassion, and only among people who are good at controlling their emotions.** Thus, the collapse of compassion may not be a basic limitation on how much compassion we can feel, but instead be due to an active choice to avoid compassion.

These findings suggest ways to defuse fear of compassion. One way would be to change people's expectations about compassion. **It may be that compassion is a limited resource only for those who *think* it is a limited resource,** so teaching people about how they can safely expand their compassion could be important. Many mindfulness – and compassion–building interventions explicitly encourage people to trust their emotions and not become distracted by fear.

Sit in a relaxed position in an upright posture.
Close your eyes and focus your attention on the sensations
of your breathing, flowing in and out. Attend to the present-moment
sensations of the in- breath and out- breath. For the next two minutes
concentrate on your breathing. If your attention wanders
elsewhere, gently guide it back to your breathing.

Next, think about the last time that someone did something
positive for you. Perhaps it was a funny joke, a special favor,
or a loving embrace. Focus on the positive emotion that you
now feel and stay with it as you breathe in and out.

As you continue to focus on this positive emotion, imagine
that you are giving this positive emotion to yourself.
It can often be difficult to have compassion for ourselves;
give the positivity to yourself with kindness and ease.

Next, imagine a small suffering child in need of help.
Imagine extending the same positivity toward this
child with kindness and ease.

Then, imagine that you are faced with a hundred
suffering children, just like this small child you imagined.
Although this might seem overwhelming to think about,
remember that fear is just a transient emotional state,
like a cloud in the sky. *Fear does not reflect reality,*
but your reaction to it. Focus on the positivity that you
have been cultivating and to your best ability,
extend it to these children with kindness and ease.

After this, return to your breathing for a few minutes.
Getting past fears of compassion can be difficult,
but remember that these fears are like clouds in the sky,
transient and passing through the mind. Trust your
compassion and its limits may be boundless.

10

"

If I let you get to know me
I might reveal things
about me that you don't like
and then I'll feel shame and
I will be with somebody
who doesn't really like me
but must be nice to me.

"

Typical Client Fear

THEME – *Overcoming Shame with Compassion: "Nature's Mind"*

I have heard this sentiment many times in therapy, especially when working with high-shame clients. People have all kinds of reasons for not letting others get too close and for not letting in compassion. The fear of being shamed is a main one.

Carrying shame within us can stop us from being compassionate with ourselves. Research has shown that some people really struggle with being open, accepting or responding to compassion from others, or even noticing it, and that many struggle with self-compassion and treating oneself kindly, especially in the context of mistakes or setbacks. There are many reasons for this.

A major fear of letting others get to know us is linked to the fear of allowing them to see what's going on in our minds. Our brains are constantly generating all kinds of fantasies, complex emotions, and intrusive images. We can have the feeling that some of these must never be known and that if people really knew what went on in our minds, we would become objects of shame and rejection.

Compassion for aches and pains and losses is doable. Compassion for the things that cause us shame is much more difficult. Yet we know that it is love and compassion that heals us; it is feeling accepted and forgiven that is the most powerful process of change within us. Compassion is a great healer of shame – we need to allow it in.

COMPASSION PRACTICE

The first meditation is to spend a few moments considering that everything that goes on in our mind, no matter what it is, it is part of being human. Our genes and our life experiences have shaped our brains to give rise to these inner experiences. This is not our fault. The more we understand this, the more compassionate we can be toward ourselves and others as we realize that we are all following the arising and flow of created desires and emotions for good or ill.

As we become mindful and observant of the mind, we become aware that this is not just "my mind" but the mind of nature – that is, as we observe the flow of thoughts and emotions like anger, worry, anxiety, sexual and other desires, we are observing "a human mind" at work; a mind created by nature. *So the first step is to not overly personalize the contents of our minds but to see them as part of our common humanity and of "nature's mind."*

The next step is to recognize that we can cultivate and choose to focus on certain parts of ourselves. So while fears, angers, and lusts will come and go very easily, we can begin to observe these without judgment or shaming but, at the same time, choose to cultivate the compassionate qualities within us and take responsibility for how we let the emotions and desires of "nature's mind" control our behavior. We can become mindful of feelings arising within us and try to hold to compassionate values by not shaming ourselves for them, but equally we can choose not to act on these feelings and find the wisdom of how to compassionately engage with that which is blocking or hurting us. The more compassionate we are with our own dark areas, the more compassionate we can be with others. Compassion then is not the road to submissive acceptance but wise engagement with that which we find difficult. And as we give up blaming and shaming ourselves we can allow others to get closer and form genuine connections with them – **we discover that we are all just human beings trying to do our best with what is actually quite a tricky brain.**

■

May I be compassionate and understanding of things about myself I don't like.

■

May I be compassionate and understanding of the things in other people I don't like.

■

May I develop wisdom and compassion for the hard things, not just for the easy things.

11

RICHARD FIELDS, PhD, chose this quote:

❝

I am the source of my own suffering, because of the habits of my mind.

❞

His Holiness the Dalai Lama

It is purported that at the age of 8, while reciting the 4 noble truths, the young Dalai Lama was told by his teacher that he was reciting with too much ego. The young prodigy reflected on this, and then uttered the above insightful quote.

How often do we allow our thoughts to ruminate to the point where a situation is escalated, resulting in anxiety, depression, and exaggerated emotional reactions? These reactive habits of our mind cause us more suffering. These habits are often driven by shame – shame that shuts down our ability to see things more clearly and allow for self-compassion. Shame is defined as the self looking in on itself and finding itself lacking, flawed, and inferior (Fossum and Mason, 1989). In her book *Radical Acceptance* (2003), Tara Brach describes shame as a "trance of unworthiness." **Shame escalates normal emotions that push away self-compassion, so anger becomes rage, and sadness becomes depression, and anxiety becomes immobilizing fear, which all contribute to feelings of unworthiness and compassion resistance.**

THEME – *Shame & Compassion Resistance*

Much like the Woody Allen line "Why would I want to join a club that would want me as a member?" the shame-based individual feels unworthy of support and compassion from others (compassion resistance), and even more unworthy of self-compassion. Their fear is that once someone gets close, they will discover this flawed person, and quickly reject and withdraw from them, causing more shame

This distorted shame-based cycle causes one to be one's own worst enemy as described in the Dalai Lama's quote. Compassion counters shame by promoting feelings of acceptance. This reminds us to interrupt the shame-based habits of our mind, quieting the voice of shame to allow for the acceptance of self-compassion and compassion from others, so that healing can occur.

COMPASSION PRACTICE

Sit in a comfortable position, and focus on your breath.

Breathe slowly, and quiet the mind. If negative thoughts arise, notice them, but let them pass, as a leaf in a stream of water. Let the breath gently push negative emotions to the center of the stream so that they can naturally be taken by the current downstream. No matter the number of negative thoughts, there is only a slight nudge necessary to float them away.

Identify someone who truly has compassion for you. Focus on their support and encouragement. Identify your own capacity to be gentle with yourself, quieting your fears and anxiety, while realizing that quieting your mind is possible. Breathe slowly and focus on your breath while accepting the compassion from this person. Repeat this process, and accept your own self-soothing and self-compassionate voice that gently reminds you that your fears will pass with time and that you are capable of self-compassion and compassion for others.

Identify someone for whom you have compassion. Focus on supporting and encouraging them. Identify your capacity to be gentle with them, helping them quiet their fears and anxiety. Give them your heartfelt compassion and notice how you feel capable of compassion, capable of goodness, and capable of living with more self-compassion.

MICHAEL D. YAPKO, PhD, chose this quote:

66

If you can talk, you can sing. If you can walk, you can dance.

99

Tribal Saying, Zimbabwe

THEME – *We are Capable of Much More*

One of the most important aspects of compassion is compassion for the self. Too often we are harsh and self-critical, creating an unkind internal environment that may diminish the vital sense of curiosity that drives exploration and personal growth. **Focusing only on what's wrong, whether with ourselves or with others, prevents us from being mindfully aware of the positive possibilities that can be hidden in even the most challenging of circumstances, thereby missing what is right, good, inspiring, and potentially healing.** I learned this quote, which shares African tribal wisdom, while talking to a tribal elder in a small village in Zimbabwe. I am moved by this powerful reminder that we can strive to be the best we can be by focusing on our strengths and on what we *can* do, rather than by focusing on our inadequacies and on what we *can't* do.

COMPASSION PRACTICE

*Each day identify and write down at least one
positive thing you did that you didn't think you could do,
perhaps surprising yourself in the nicest of ways.
For example, you may have felt rushed and pressed for time
but still stopped and patiently offered some form
of assistance to someone. Or, you felt the initial surge
of anger with someone, yet responded kindly and respectfully.
Or, you felt unmotivated to do something that you simply
didn't want to do, yet did it and did it well.
From these observations of surpassing your own
initial expectations, you can begin to discover
your strengths and appreciate them with a gentle compassion
towards yourself. To extend this toward others,
notice and write down at least one thing per day
you observed someone else do that clearly required
a higher sense of self. If appropriate, make a point of generously
acknowledging what you observed directly to that person.*

Kindness

13

ROSHI JOAN HALIFAX, PhD, chose this quote:

It is above all by the imagination that we achieve perception and compassion and hope.

Ursula K. Le Guin, National Book Award Acceptance Speech, *1973*

THEME – *Kindness: The Grace of Compassion*

Someone once told me that kindness is the grace of compassion. It is one of the ways we express our love and nonduality in relation to each other. Kindness is a quality of great value for our work on behalf of those who are suffering. **How can we give care without kindness? Of course, kindness needs to be there, or our care is cold and mechanical, defensive or shrunken with fear, tentative and distracted.**

COMPASSION PRACTICE

This practice is from the Tibetan Buddhist tradition. The practice is so simple, and yet may be one of the hardest things we can do. It is a practice of ultimate and extreme compassion, a brave act of love when we see through the eyes of another.

First remember why you are practicing.

Recall your aspiration for this vow to really be of benefit to others, for this vow to awaken you from your own suffering.

Let your practice rest in the hands of your good heart as you remember your innermost request.

Now, bring to your mind and heart the presence of someone who is suffering deeply. Maybe this one is sitting before you now.

Open your heart and mind to this one.

Feel your way into this one's heart.

Look out through his or her eyes.

Really imagine that you are this person, living their life, feeling their suffering, and knowing this one's heart.

Be this one.

Feel into how they experience their world, their life.

Exchange yourself for this one.

Spend time being this one.

After some time has passed, let yourself rest in unconditioned presence.

End the practice by dedicating the merit to the well-being of others.

14

ELISHA GOLDSTEIN, PhD, chose this quote:

"

Be kind whenever possible. It is always possible.

"

His Holiness the Dalai Lama

THEME – *Being Kind*

When we look at this quote we have to really ask, is it really always possible to have compassion? When someone cuts you off on the highway or another person has 14 items in the 10 items or less express line, is kindness possible? Or how about when we're feeling particularly stressed, anxious, or depressed, is compassion even possible then? Or when someone is abusive toward you?

Many would argue that the doorway to happiness is to a life geared toward kindness and compassion.

However, compassion does not mean that you have to agree with what someone is doing or even be tolerant of it. Accepting verbal or physical abuse is certainly not compassionate toward yourself.

Fundamentally, we need to learn how to be kind to ourselves. Many of us find that the most difficult practice of all. That is why in the practice of cultivating compassion, we begin with ourselves.

More often than not when I ask people all the things they have to do that day, there is a long list. When I then ask, "And where are you on this list?" a quizzical facial expression forms as if I were speaking a tongue from another planet. Whatever the reason, we're just not kind to ourselves and that makes it difficult to spread that kindness to others.

Compassion is often contagious and if a few more of us were infected by it, we would have more nurturing environments at home, work, and in public places.

The bottom line is that compassion is considered a strength in many traditions, including the field of psychology. It can also be nurtured formally and through little acts during the day.

So is it always possible? Well, we can hold that as an aspiration or as the light to guide our intention. **However, if it is too difficult sometimes, don't pressure yourself too much. Just come back to it when you can with intention and notice how you feel overall.** Most of all, don't just take the Dalai Lama's word for it, try it out for yourself and see how it goes.

COMPASSION PRACTICE

Making Compassion Part of Daily Life:

Set an intention for today to look for moments where you are aware of either yourself or another suffering.

In that moment, ask yourself if it is possible to respond with kindness. If so, act with kindness.

See how you feel after the act is completed. At the end of the day, we always want our experience to be our teacher.

As you intentionally practice and repeat it, you'll notice more moments of grace like this falling in on you throughout the day.

15

SUSAN KAISER GREENLAND, JD, chose this quote:

There is such a thing
as raw, unalloyed,
agendaless kindness.

David Foster Wallace, Infinite Jest, *1996*

THEME – *Compassion: Random Acts of Agendaless Kindness*

What draws me to this line from David Foster Wallace's iconic book *Infinite Jest* is its incredulous tone. "There is such a thing as raw, unalloyed, agendaless kindness" is just one of almost ten pages of "exotic new facts" that the narrator of *Infinite Jest* learns during his time in a substance recovery facility. The exotic new facts are written in tone that suggests that all of them are surprising, including the existence of raw, unalloyed, agendaless kindness.

It turns out that the narrator of *Infinite Jest* isn't the only one who feels this way. A recent study looking at the effect of random acts of kindness on both the giver and receiver found that many people are suspicious of kind gestures. What do they want from me? What is his or her agenda? But regardless of the receiver's mindset, emerging research in the areas of positive psychology and altruism indicate that **spontaneous acts of kindness are good for the health and well-being of the giver.**

Kindness connects us with others in our communities and often we begin to see positive qualities in those to whom we are kind that we haven't seen before.

Kindness boosts our image of ourselves as we tend to see ourselves as altruistic and generous.

Kindness can ignite a chain reaction of kindness. Our acts inspire others to be kind as well.

Genuine kindness requires us to focus on the goodness and wisdom of what we're doing rather than on the result and the less we focus on the result the better we tend to feel. Not surprisingly, that's another of the exotic new facts discovered by Wallace's narrator in *Infinite Jest*: "That if you do something nice for somebody in secret, anonymously… it's almost its own form of intoxicating buzz."

Acts of raw, unalloyed, agendaless kindness needn't be grand or flamboyant. The most powerful ones often seem small and are targeted to help someone else with something specific: offering jumper cables to a stranger whose car battery needs a charge, for instance, or helping another passenger lift a heavy bag into the overhead bin on an airplane. We can integrate spontaneous acts of kindness into every day of our lives, but, like everything else, it takes a little practice.

*Choose a friend, colleague or other person in your life
who you feel relatively neutral toward – we're going to
call this person your "Secret Friend." This week reflect
(and sometimes act) on the following prompts:*

*On Sunday, notice something you have in common with
your secret friend and jot your reflections down in a journal.*

*On Monday, notice something that's different
and jot your reflections down in a journal.*

*On Tuesday, notice something you really like
about the person, something you admire or aspire towards,
and jot your reflections down in a journal.*

*On Wednesday, silently (and secretly) send loving kindness
to your secret friend and notice what comes up in your mind
and body in response. Jot your reflections down in a journal.*

*On Thursday, consider whether there is anything
about your secret friend that bugs you, or that you think
would annoy you were you to spend much time with him or her.
Jot those reflections down in a journal, if you have a chance.*

*On Friday, give your secret friend a compliment
based on something real and tangible, in other words,
a compliment that comes from what you learned this week reflecting
on his or her qualities. Jot those reflections down in a journal too.*

*On Saturday, offer a seemingly random act of kindness
to your secret friend. It doesn't have to be a grand gesture –
it can be something small like clearing his or her plate
after a meal or carrying his or her grocery bag to the car if it's heavy.
Again, if you have a moment, jot down your reflections.*

50 ■ Section III

16

SHARON SALZBERG chose this quote:

66

If you knew as I did the power of giving, you would not let a single meal pass without sharing something.

99

The Buddha

THEME – *Kindness & The Power of Giving*

Generosity is a matter of spirit. It has little to do with whether or not we have material goods to give or don't. There is always something that we can give to another, for giving is our heart's offering of connection and caring.

In India and Burma I was the recipient of incredible generosity from many people who had very little materially to offer. Yet when they gave, they did so wholeheartedly. People there taught me about generosity, and showed me that it doesn't depend on conventional, external abundance. And if we cannot offer something material, we can give energetically: a smile, or our full, undistracted attention.

The Buddha said that no true spiritual life is possible without this kind of generous heart. Generosity is the very first quality of an awakened mind because of the beautiful quality of joy that arises in an act of true giving. Giving is a happy thing to do. We experience happiness in forming the intention to give, in the actual act of giving and in the recollection of the fact that we have given. Generosity has been one of my own important personal practices because it reminds me of the capacity of my own heart to go beyond fear ("What if I need that book next week? What if I'm not giving enough?") to honor the power of connection.

COMPASSION PRACTICE

This is a practice that helps cultivate generosity through awareness:
If a strong impulse to give something arises in your mind
and it won't cause any harm (like giving away your family's rent money),
then make the offering. Stay aware of what is arising in your mind,
especially if the next fifty thoughts following the intention
to give are fearful, like: "Maybe I'll wear it next year";
"Maybe I will read it after all"; "What if they think
I'm stupid for doing this?" Let the thoughts go
as you remember your motivation, and remember
*that **generosity is actually a practice, one that implies***
intentionality, challenges and venturing into new terrain.
Stay aware of your thoughts and feelings after the act of generosity.
Are you in fact regretful? Relieved? Buoyant?
Let your insights guide your ongoing practice of generosity.

Self-Compassion

17

CHRIS GERMER, PhD, chose this quote:

For someone to develop genuine
compassion towards others,
first he or she must have a basis
upon which to cultivate compassion,
and that basis is the ability
to connect to one's own feelings
and to care for one's own welfare...
Caring for others requires
caring for oneself.

His Holiness the Dalai Lama,
www.dalailama.com/teachings/training-the-mind/verse-7,
excerpted from, Transforming the Mind, *2000*

THEME – *Self-Compassion Increases our Capacity for Compassion for Others*

Self-compassion is a healthy response to one's own suffering, much as we'd respond to someone whom we truly love. As the Dalai Lama points out, it's the foundation of caring for others, for how can we cherish in others what we find distasteful in ourselves.

There are a variety of misunderstandings about self-compassion that interfere with giving ourselves the kindness we need. For example, self-compassion is often confused with self-indulgence, self-pity, or self-absorption. The research shows precisely the opposite. **Self-compassion is unrelated to narcissism and self-compassionate people tend to feel more connected and compassionate toward others. Furthermore, turning toward ourselves with kindness when we suffer, fail, or feel inadequate decreases anxiety and depression and enhances emotional resilience.**

Why the persistent bias against self-compassion, even among Buddhist scholars? The underlying fear seems to be that the "self" in self-compassion subtly reinforces the illusion of separation. The Buddha was very clear that "selfing" is the cause of most emotional suffering. We spend our entire lives promoting and protecting our "selves" against real or imagined danger, entirely missing the miracle of life unfolding in and around us. For example, neuroimaging research demonstrates that the brain reverts to a "default mode" when it's in a resting state, which typically means rumination about personal problems that occurred in the past or could occur in the future. We certainly don't want to add any practices to our lives that compound our suffering by strengthening the sense of a fixed, separate self. Which begs the question: "When should we direct compassion toward ourselves and when toward others?"

The litmus test of self-compassion seems to be whether it leads to more or less "selfing." **If a warm, tender attitude toward ourselves decreases rumination and allows us to connect with others, it's probably a good thing. When we feel reasonably good, then focusing on the needs of others might provide still greater emotional freedom and joy.**

COMPASSION PRACTICE

Set your mind to be aware when you're under stress, perhaps 3-4 times per day. When stress occurs, put your hand over your heart and say to yourself, "May I be happy and free from suffering." Notice how you feel. Then focus on a person who may be involved in your stressful situation, put your hand over your heart and say, "May you be happy and free from suffering." How do you feel now? Note which practice brought you the most emotional freedom.

18

KRISTIN NEFF, PhD, chose this quote:

The curious paradox is that when I accept myself just as I am, then I can change.

Carl Rogers, On Becoming a Person: A Therapist's View of Psychotherapy, *1961*

THEME – *Quieting the Self-Critic: Imperfection is Part of the Shared Human Experience*

I come back to this quote again and again because it so nicely captures the paradoxical nature of growth that occurs by practicing self-compassion. Many people are puzzled by the idea that we should accept ourselves as we are. Why? I'm a mess! Why would I want to accept myself? I want to change, and need to criticize myself in order to do so.

Self-criticism is not a useful motivator of change. Research shows that self-critics are much more likely to be anxious and depressed – mind states that can interfere with taking the steps needed for change. They also have less self-confidence, which undermines their potential for success. The habit of self-criticism engenders fear of failure, meaning that self-critics often don't even try to achieve their goals because the possibility of failure is unacceptable. Even more problematic, self-critics have a hard time seeing themselves clearly and identifying needed areas of improvement because they know the self-punishment that will ensue if they admit the truth. Much better to deny there's a problem or, even better, blame it on someone else.

But is a compassionate response to our shortcomings any better? Yes.

It's relatively easy to see when we think about how a compassionate and caring parent might motivate a child who is struggling. Let's say your teenage daughter Mary comes home from school with a failing math grade. If you say, "You're so stupid and lame! What a loser! You're hopeless and will never amount to anything!" is that really going to help motivate Mary? Instead it will probably depress her to the point of wanting to give up math all together. Much more effective would be to take an understanding and supportive approach: "I know you're disappointed, and clearly something is not working in your study routine. But I know you can do it. How can I help and support you?" This compassionate approach is much more likely to give Mary the emotional resources needed to pick herself up and try again.

It's exactly the same when we take a caring and compassionate approach with ourselves. Compassion is concerned with the alleviation of suffering. When we feel compassion for our own pain – especially when the pain comes from our maladaptive habits and behaviors – we want to heal our pain. We want to make changes and improvements that will help us suffer less. **Self-compassion also allows us to more clearly acknowledge areas of personal weakness by recognizing that imperfection is part of the shared human experience.** We can then work on improving ourselves, not because we're unacceptable as we are, but because we want to thrive and be happy.

*Here's an exercise that can help you motivate change
with self-acceptance rather than self-judgment.*

1. *Think about a personal trait for which you
harshly criticize yourself (such as being negative, moody,
overweight, etc.) and that you would like to change.*

2. *Try to get in touch with the emotional pain
that your self-criticism causes, giving yourself compassion
for the experience of feeling so judged. Remind yourself
that you're only human, imperfect, just like the rest of us,
with weakness as well as strengths.*

3. *Put your hand over your heart and repeat the phrase
"May I be kind to myself. May I accept myself as I am."*

4. *Next, ask yourself what would a caring friend,
parent, or partner say to gently encourage you
to make a change, while also reminding you of their
unconditional love and acceptance? What is the most
supportive message this person could give you?*

5. *Put your hand over your heart again and
repeat these words of caring encouragement to yourself.*

**You'll be much more likely to blossom by watering the seeds
of self-acceptance rather than of self-criticism.**

19

ELISHA GOLDSTEIN, PhD, chose this quote:

66

I'm afraid some times you'll play lonely games too. Games you can't win 'cause you'll play against you.

99

Dr. Suess, Oh, the Places You'll Go!, *1990*

THEME – *Self-Compassion Counters Self-Limiting Beliefs*

Somewhere deep inside our brain, still yet to be located by science, lives a part of us that serves to sabotage our best laid aspirations. **This area of the brain is the keeper of our limiting beliefs and it seems to know exactly when to let them out. It tells us what we "can't" do, what's wrong with us, and puts a ceiling on possibility.** When it shouts its bad advice, we get instantly hooked and begin arguing with it. Now there are two voices in our heads warring against one another and ultimately we are the casualties.

The experience of being beat down by or battling with our limiting beliefs is something that happens automatically to all of us. It drudges up painful feelings of unworthiness and shame. Ultimately, we come up with ways to escape this pain that are often unhealthy. We find a variety of "false" refuges to make us feel better by tuning out with our technology, shutting down emotionally, excessive shopping, overspending, overeating, or other even more destructive habits like drug and alcohol abuse, or compulsive gambling.

In one of these difficult moments it's natural and adaptive to seek healing. A healthier way to do this is through self-compassion. **Self-compassion is when we understand that we're experiencing something painful and we are inclined to support ourselves.**

While in the past you may have been playing *against* yourself, you now can start playing in *favor* of yourself.

It's a good practice to get to know what our common limiting beliefs are that keep us stuck. Consider yours. Is it that you believe that you are unlovable? Or, that you won't find a healing path to working with your anxiety, depression or trauma? Getting a sense of what these limiting beliefs are can help prime our minds to recognize them when they arise.

While you may not be able to control the forming of these thoughts, with awareness you can choose how to respond to them. One of the most skillful and healing ways is through self-compassion.

In one of these difficult moments, if all you did was to put your hand on your heart and wish yourself well, this would be a moment well spent.

Implement a 5-Step Compassion Practice:

1. *Make a list of your "Top 5 Limiting Beliefs."*
Be on the lookout for them in the coming day or week.

2. *When one arises, see if you can connect to the emotion*
that arises with it. Is it shame, anger, disgust,
or maybe sadness? Get a sense of how this feels in the body
and see it as your own inner child.

3. *Ask yourself what does this part of you need?*

4. *Place your hand on your heart and wish this part of you*
well, to be safe, to be healthy, and to be free from fear.

5. *Take note of the feeling as if you were putting a frame*
around it, imprinting a healing memory.

20

PAUL GILBERT, PhD, chose this quote:

"
I never beat myself up gently.
"

Patient's saying

THEME – *A Friendly Self-Compassionate Voice*

Many years ago, when I was practicing therapy, I discovered that the way people tried to help themselves was often to be critical, harsh, and even bullying. "Come on, you idiot, stop thinking this way. Pull yourself together. You're making things worse. You're making mountains out of molehills. You should know better than this, etc." So I developed a very simple intervention to help people create an internal, kind voice. **If you practice every day hearing your own voice in your head (as you do when you think), textured with understanding, kindness, and support, this will help you in your times of difficulty.**

COMPASSION PRACTICE

Sit quietly in a chair for a moment and slow the breath to prepare the body. Now, for about 15-30 seconds just stay with the facial expression you have right now, which is probably neutral. Notice how that feels – pay attention to your facial muscles. Then, for 15-30 seconds create a friendly facial expression, as if you're with somebody you really like being with – a kind of joyful friendliness. Then go back to a neutral face for 15-30 seconds and then back to a friendly face, so that you've done each exercise twice. Reflect and compare and contrast what happens to your body and your feelings when you deliberately change facial expressions. What did you notice? What happens if you sit for a while just slowing the breath gently and focusing on a gentle, friendly facial expression – nothing too exaggerated or forced, just very gentle?

Next, we're going to generate a friendly thinking tone. On the out-breath simply say "hello" to yourself – and name yourself. So in my case it would be, "Hello Paul." Do this for about 15-30 seconds on the out-breath with a neutral tone in your voice. It is a "hello" that is relatively indifferent – sort of factual. Notice how it feels. Then, for the same amount of time, create a friendly voice, as if you are speaking to somebody you really like being with and are expressing your friendliness to him/her. It's a very welcoming tone. Practice different kinds of voices, until you get one that sounds really friendly and supportive and comfortable. Then, go back to neutral voice for about 15-30 seconds and notice what happens to your feelings. Finally, finish with a friendly voice. Now, for the next minute or two, practice just sitting with this idea of the inner friendly and compassionate voice.

Try to practice this every day for at least a minute – longer if you can – generating compassionate expressions and voice tones. The point here is to remember that this is important to do. So even if you practice for just a minute each day, at least you have acknowledged each day that paying attention to the emotional tone and textures of your thinking is very important. Note if your thoughts tend towards ruminating about things that anger you, if they take on an angry tone or maybe an anxious tone. When you think about yourself, what is the emotional tone of your thoughts? Try to create, on purpose, friendly, supportive, and wise tones. If you are troubled, spend a moment to slow the breath and ground the body and bring your compassionate inner voice to this moment.

21

KRISTIN NEFF, PhD, chose this quote:

66

Compassion is not a relationship between the healer and the wounded. It's a relationship between equals. Only when we know our own darkness well can we be present with the darkness of others. Compassion becomes real when we recognize our shared humanity.

99

Pema Chödrön, The Places That Scare You: A Guide to Fearlessness in Difficult Times, *2001*

THEME – *Self-Compassion: Putting Personal Inadequacies (Our Own Darkness) in Perspective*

One of the most important elements of self-compassion is the recognition of our shared humanity. Compassion is, by definition, relational. Compassion literally means "to suffer with," which implies a basic mutuality in the experience of suffering. The emotion of compassion springs from the recognition that the human experience is imperfect, that we are all fallible. **When we're in touch with our common humanity, we remember that feelings of inadequacy and disappointment are universal.** This is what distinguishes self-compassion from self-pity. While self-pity says "poor me," self-compassion recognizes that suffering is part of the shared human experience. The pain I feel in difficult times is the same pain that you feel in difficult times. The triggers are different, the circumstances are different, the degree of pain is different, but the basic experience is the same.

Recognizing common humanity also allows us to be more understanding and less judgmental about our inadequacies. Our thoughts, feelings, and actions are largely impacted by factors outside of our control: parenting history, culture, genetic and environmental conditions, as well as the demands and expectations of others. After all, if we had full control over our behavior, how many people would consciously choose to have anger problems, addiction issues, debilitating social anxiety, or an eating disorder? Many aspects of our selves and the circumstances of our lives are not of our own choosing, but instead stem from innumerable factors that are outside our sphere of influence. When we acknowledge this reality, our difficulties do not have to be taken so personally. We can embrace ourselves and others with compassion, rather than blame.

*Think about a trait that you often judge yourself for,
and that is an important part of your self-definition.
For example, you may think of yourself as a shy person, lazy,
angry, etc. Then ask yourself the following questions:*

1. *How often do you display this trait – most of the time,
sometimes, only occasionally? Who are you when
you don't display the trait – are you still you?*

2. *Are you the only person who displays this trait,
or is this a common human experience?*

3. *What are the various causes and conditions that led
to having the trait in the first place (early family
experiences, genetics, life pressures, etc.)?
If these "outside" forces were partly responsible for
you having this trait, is it accurate to think
of the trait as reflecting the inner you?*

4. *What happens when you reframe your self-description
so that you are not defining yourself in terms of the trait?
For example, instead of saying, "I am an angry person,"
what happens when you say, "sometimes, in certain
circumstances, I get angry." By identifying less strongly
with this trait, does anything change? Can you sense
any more space, freedom, and peace of mind?*

22

AMY WEINTRAUB, MFA, ERYT-500, chose this quote:

> **My beloved Child, break your heart no longer. Each time you judge yourself you break your own heart.**

Swami Kripalvananda

THEME – *Self-Compassion: Quieting the "Inner Critic"*

How many hundreds of yoga classes did I teach, quoting my teacher at the end of each class, before my heart's mind understood those words? Why did saying them to my students still bring tears to my eyes? Why, after years of meditation, therapy, and medication, was I still so mean to myself? Before I began a daily yoga practice in the late 1980s, no amount of meditation turned the volume down on that monster in my mind. Every one of us has an inner critic. Mark Twain said that if we talked to our children the way we talk to ourselves, we would be arrested for child abuse. I was particularly hard on myself in the 1970s after my marriage failed. Had anyone been listening to my self-abuse, they would have locked me up and thrown away the key.

My secret name for myself was "Amy Shamey." **Shame wasn't just a thought or belief. It wasn't just an emotion. It was a part of my physical being, a daily visceral experience that whooshed through my body, bringing waves of heat, a feeling of humiliation and with it, grief.** No amount of talking about it in therapy, watching it arise on the meditation cushion, or numbing it out with meds, touched the core of my self-hatred. Of course, my body image had a lot to do with it. I saw myself as chubby, unattractive, and clumsy, compared to my beautiful mother, whose expressive face appeared on the covers of magazines like *True Confessions* and *Romance* in the late 1940s. My body was not my friend. It had an embarrassing plumpness in the places that should have been lean and an embarrassing flatness in the places that should have been round. From this description, you might think I wasn't pretty. We're talking about self-image here, not reality. Pictures attest to my cuteness as a kid and my downright beauty in my teens. I don't think my creative dance teacher would have tried to convince my mother when I was eleven to enroll me in a proper ballet studio with daily classes if she hadn't seen in me a grace and fluidity I couldn't see in myself. But whatever the source, I hated my body and nearly everything else that went by the name of Amy.

So what changed? In the late 1980s, I made my first visit to Kripalu Center in Stockbridge, Massachusetts and took my first yoga class. Despite meditating since the early 1970s and practicing a bit of yoga asana, it wasn't until that first visit to Kripalu that a teacher spoke the words attributed to Swami Kripalvananda, "My beloved child, break your heart no longer. Each time you judge yourself, you break your own heart." I am sure I wept on my mat when I heard them, although I don't remember. What I do remember is emerging from the class feeling a sense of spacious abundance, a touching into wholeness that I had never experienced before. In those moments after class, it didn't matter what I looked like or what mistakes I may have made in my life. I had touched something deep within me that was absolutely perfect, just as it was. In those moments after class, there was nothing I needed to fix, no way I needed to change.

I left Kripalu with a commitment to practicing yoga every day. After each morning of stretching and breathing and staying present to the physical sensations the poses evoked, I felt more at home in my body. I rose from my mat feeling at ease with the Amy who looked back at me from the mirror.

The self-judgment didn't immediately cease in the hours I spent off the mat, but eventually the daily whoosh of shame became weekly, then monthly, and then it disappeared altogether. If my inner critic attacked, I found myself talking back instead of believing everything she said. When I rolled out my mat to practice, her voice fell silent. When I made a mistake or fell short of my own expectations, she always had something to say, but I didn't necessarily believe her anymore. By the early 1990s, I was teaching a workshop at Kripalu called *Befriending Your Inner Critic*, leading others in exercises to find compassion for themselves, including their shame parts and their nasty inner critics. From that workshop, I offer you a compassion practice.

COMPASSION PRACTICE

Spend a week with this compassion practice and watch your compassion for all your parts begin to outshine the weakening voice of your inner critic. Part One is a practice of breathing while moving that, in addition to bringing in more fresh oxygen and releasing old carbon dioxide from your lungs, provides an opportunity to be fully aware of and be present to physical sensations. This sensory awareness is the portal into the moving meditation we will do in Part Two that offers compassion to places in your body. You can do each practice by itself, but it works best to put them together.

Part One: Power Hara Breath

1. *Stand with your feet slightly wider than hip width apart and bring hands to your shoulders with your elbows pointed out like chicken wings.*

2. *Inhale, filling your lungs halfway as you twist to the left.*

3. *Inhale fully as you twist to the right.*

4. *Extend your right arm forcefully to the left as you twist to the left, exhaling through your mouth with a vigorous "ha" sound.*

5. *Extend your left arm forcefully to the right as you twist to the right, exhaling again through your mouth with a "ha" sound.*

6. *Practice five to ten full rounds. Release and stand with your eyes closed and your palms open. Sense deeply into your face, feel the sensation in your face, your arms, the palms of your hands. Sense the tingling in your palms.*

Part Two: "Be still beloved, and know that you are safely held."

1. *Let your right hand nest in your left hand with the tips of your thumbs touching and say to yourself, "Be still, beloved hands and know that you are safely held."*

2. *Bounce on your feet for about thirty seconds. Stop and feel the sensation in your feet. Say to yourself, "Be still, beloved feet and know that you are safely held."*

3. *Now find a comfortable seated position or lie down on the floor. Repeat the phrase, moving through your body, like this: "Be still beloved (body part)," as you inhale; "and know that you are safely held," as you exhale.*

4. *Begin with the left foot. "Be still beloved left foot," as you inhale; "and know that you are safely held," as you exhale. Repeat this phrase as you move up the left side of your body, all the way up to your crown. As you speak to your head, you might wish to place your hands on your head so your little fingers are touching at your hairline and your index fingers point to your crown.*

5. *Do the same practice, beginning with the right foot and moving up the right side of your body.*

6. *Speak to your torso, including your buttocks, genitals, belly, chest, spine, and breasts. Feel free to place your hands on each body part as you speak to it.*

End by placing your right hand on your heart, and your left hand on top, linking your thumbs in a hand gesture called eagle mudra. End with the phrase, **"Be still beloved heart, and know that you are safely held."**

23

SHAUNA L. SHAPIRO, PhD, chose this quote:

66

You can search
throughout the entire
universe for someone
who is more deserving of
your love and affection
than you are yourself.

99

The Buddha

THEME – *Self-Compassion & Self-Love*

In this quote the Buddha offers the radical teaching that each of us is deserving of self-compassion and self-love. We are often taught that it is important to have compassion and to love thy neighbor as thyself. And yet, when we look closely at our own "self-compassion" and "self-love" we often find it is painfully lacking. Some years ago, one of my teachers invited me to reflect deeply on my relationship to myself. She asked, "Do you love yourself? Do you have compassion for yourself?" And when I reflected upon this I was unsure. She suggested that I begin to say each day, "I love you Shauna. I have compassion for you, Shauna," and to try to feel and embody this. I looked at her as if she were crazy, and flat out said, "No, that's not the practice for me. It feels too forced and airy-fairy and I'm not sure it is authentic." She gently conceded, and offered a different practice, "How about simply saying, "Good morning, Shauna.""

"Yes" I replied, "that I can do." I had recently divorced and I would often wake up in the morning feeling sad and alone. Now, when I woke up, I began to say, "Good morning, Shauna," and I felt the kindness and self-compassion in this simple morning greeting. After a few months, my teacher asked how the good morning practice was going. I shared how natural it had become and that I was actually enjoying it. "It sounds like you have graduated," she responded with a soft smile. "Your next practice is to say, "Good morning, I love and have compassion for you, Shauna.""

And then one morning, I felt "it." I actually felt love and compassion for myself pouring through me. Tears filled my eyes as I poignantly realized that I was experiencing self-love and self-compassion for the first time that I could remember. I felt so vulnerable and raw. I also felt so grateful and so alive.

I would like to say these feelings of self-love and self-compassion now pervade my every moment of lived experience and that I float through life encapsulated in a soft white light of unconditional self-love and self-compassion. This is not the case. However, I can say that the pattern of self-love and self-compassion, once created, has never ceased to exist. It is something I can return to and remember over and over again. The American author and physician Oliver Wendell Holmes wrote that **"a mind once stretched…never regains its original dimensions." I would add that a heart once stretched never regains it original dimensions.**

1. *Reflect upon the Buddha's teaching:*

*"You can search throughout the entire universe
for someone who is more deserving of your love
and affection than you are yourself."*

*Do you believe this? What would it feel like
to let yourself believe this, just as an experiment?*

2. *Each day when you wake up, greet yourself with
"Good morning (your name)." And if you are really
brave try saying "Good morning, I love you (your name).
Good morning, I have compassion for you (your name)."*

*I invite you to try saying this in different tones of voice,
softly, loudly, whispering it, silently... See what feels
most authentic and what most resonates in your body.*

*Play with it. Add movement or physical touch
to the words. I found that putting my hand over my heart
when I greeted myself significantly increased
the felt sense of love and compassion.*

3. *Share your experience with one dear friend,
and invite them to do the practice with you.
Each morning you will say,
"Good morning, I love you (your name).
Good morning, I have compassion for you (your name)."*

*Then say to each other in turn,
"Good morning, I love you (your friend's name).
Good morning I have compassion for you (your friend's name)."*

Quotes № 24 to 31

Interconnectedness

24

ROSHI JOAN HALIFAX, PhD, chose this quote:

Love and compassion are necessities, not luxuries. Without them humanity cannot survive.

His Holiness the Dalai Lama

THEME – *Compassion is a Necessity*

Compassion is a precious necessity for all of us. **We all need to cultivate compassion in our lives. It is one of our most treasured social assets and nourishes the human heart**, plus it is good for others. What would our world be without compassion? How could we live without compassion? What would our world be with more compassion? Compassion in our schools, in our government, in our hospitals, in our media? Why don't we vote based on compassion? Why don't we train our kids in compassion? **I want to live in a world where compassion is valued, don't you?**

COMPASSION PRACTICE

First find a quiet moment, a quiet space. Let your heart and mind settle. Then recall someone to whom you feel especially close, someone whom you deeply wish to be free of suffering, whether the suffering is physical, social, mental, or spiritual.

As you experience how this might feel, breathe deeply into your belly and track whatever you are sensing physically.

Recall that person's humanness and good qualities, as well as the suffering that he or she has been through or is going through.

Now internally repeat simple phrases of compassion toward the person you have visualized. With your breath, silently say to him or her:

May you be free from this suffering.
May you be safe.
May you find peace.

Continue to visualize this person as you breathe and silently say to him or her:

May you be free from this suffering.
May you be safe.
May you find peace.

And for a final time, visualizing your friend or relative silently and sincerely say to him or her:

May you be free from this suffering.
May you be safe.
May you find peace.

Let your wish for this one person help strengthen your aspiration to help others.

25

> A human being is a part of the whole, called by us 'Universe,' a part limited in time and space. He experiences himself, his thoughts and feelings as something separated from the rest, a kind of optical delusion of his consciousness. This delusion is a kind of prison for us, restricting us to our personal desires and to affection for a few persons nearest to us. Our task must be to free ourselves from this prison by widening our circle of compassion to embrace all living creatures and the whole of nature in its beauty. Nobody is able to achieve this completely, but the striving for such achievement is in itself a part of the liberation and a foundation for inner security.

Albert Einstein

THEME – *Loving Kindness for All*

This beautiful quote is particularly stunning for me because it reflects the wisdom of a Western scientist rather than an Eastern spiritual teacher. Perhaps it is because of my near total lack of understanding of mathematics and Einstein's theory of relativity, but I did not expect a Nobel Prize scientist to have such sentiments! When I encountered this quote, I found it expressed with such haunting beauty the deep experience of inter-connectedness. You can sense that it is based upon direct experiential awareness rather than formulaic reasoning.

Metta, or loving kindness, means to radiate out from a constricted focus on the "Self" as separate from the "Other," from "Me" and "Mine" to "Us" and "Everyone." What a huge task this is for us to achieve! It requires persistent practice, working against our biological nature.

Ironically, our spiritual nature is often most available during times of threat, crisis, and suffering rather than times of good fortune and material plentitude. I have marveled at this after many years of working with prisoners who often live under dire and dangerous conditions. Their minds are ready to explore the most fundamental existential issues of survival, peace, and happiness. In the midst of this deepened awareness of self, they can expand their circle to others.

My concern is that the world is rapidly becoming more distracted and self-centered. As prisoners like to say, **"The only way out is in."** This wisdom gained from those within the belly of the beast of incarceration can remind us to practice loving kindness.

COMPASSION PRACTICE

Sit in a comfortable position. Let your mind be still. Focus on the breath. Hold an image or sense the presence of all those to whom you are sending selfless love and good wishes. Feel the metta *coming from your heart and moving forth into the universe.*

May all beings be filled with loving kindness.
May all beings be well.
May all beings be peaceful and at ease.
May all beings be happy.

26

SHAUNA L. SHAPIRO, PhD, chose this quote:

The fundamental delusion of humanity is to suppose that I am here and you are out there.

Yasutani Hakuun Roshi (1885-1973)

THEME – *Interconnection*

Compassion is our birthright. It is the natural response of a wise and open heart. When our minds are clear and we are able to see the truth of our interconnectedness, the only appropriate response is one of helping compassion. For example, let's say that the left hand has a splinter in it. The right hand would naturally pull out the splinter, right? The left hand wouldn't say to the right hand, "Oh, thank you so much! You're so compassionate and generous!" The right hand removing the splinter is simply the appropriate response – it's just what the right hand does, because the two hands are part of the same body.

The more we practice mindful awareness, the more we begin to see that we are all part of the same body – that "I," as the right hand, actually feel "you", the left hand's pain, and I naturally want to help. Mindfulness cultivates this interconnectedness and clear seeing, which leads to greater compassion and understanding of the mysterious web in which we all are woven. No one and no thing are separate. As Chief Seattle reminds us, "Humankind has not woven the web of life. We are but one thread within it. Whatever we do to the web, we do to ourselves. All things are bound together. All things connect."

And so we begin to see that compassion isn't about being "good" or being "nice." Compassion is about seeing clearly and simply doing the only thing that makes sense. If I have a splinter in one hand, the other hand takes it out. If I see a person or a nation suffering, my wisdom and compassion catalyze the natural human response to help alleviate this suffering. The Dalai Lama states that "the suffering of one person or one nation is the suffering of humanity. That the happiness of one person or nation is the happiness of humanity." Our compassion is not for someone else, that poor person over there separate from me. Compassion is felt for all of us because we are all in this together.

COMPASSION PRACTICE

Sit quietly and comfortably, connecting gently with the body and the breath. Invite in an intention to see clearly the interconnectedness of all things. Feel the wholesomeness of your intention and your dedication to cultivate greater wisdom and compassion. Let this intention nourish and motivate you.

Behold each other silently and relax your body. Allow the breath to be natural. Notice how it feels to be in the presence of another, to offer your full awareness. Recognize that he or she is unique, different from anyone else. Stay connected with your own body, keeping 70% of you attention here, even as you

gaze upon and feel this being. Feel them
through your own sense gates.

As you behold this person, open your awareness
to their strengths and their potentialities.
In this being are reserves of courage and intelligence
and compassion. See the beauty here and also see
the sorrow here. Open your awareness to the pain
this person may have experienced in her life. In all human
lives there are sorrows, disappointments, and losses.
As you open to the suffering, know that you cannot
take it away, but you can be with it. Feel your caring
for this person, and your desire for them to be free
from fear, free from sorrow, and from the causes
of suffering. Know that what you are now
experiencing is compassion, known as Karuna *in Buddhism.*

27

"

Compassion is sometimes the fatal capacity for feeling what it is like to live inside somebody else's skin. It is the knowledge that there can never really be any peace and joy for me until there is peace and joy finally for you too.

"

Frederick Buechner

THEME – *We Are Not Separate, but Inter-"twined"*

This quote expresses a deep truth for me – the clear knowledge that compassion naturally arises when we realize that we are not separate from anyone or anything. We have to make a vow to keep our hearts open to the suffering of others, who are not really others. This kind of **radical empathy** can be painful. As Buechner says, it can even be fatal. We can react to this pain by trying to escape from it or by arguing with the circumstances and, more subtly, by creating an artificial separation between "them" and "us."

Earlier this year I experienced a period fraught with unusual events, some joyful, some not so much. High winds and rain from hurricanes had disrupted life in many ways. One small event that happened again and again at the Zen Temple where I live was the fall of one particular string of Tibetan prayer flags. Our city has an ordinance against street signs on our residential block, and so we use the prayer flags (as well as a huge granite Buddha statue) to signal our presence to the world as a Zen Buddhist temple. (I have heard some remarks that the flags also make our parking lot look a little bit like a car dealership, but this is a minority opinion.)

One day, with winds blowing strong, I was attempting to put up the flags once again. It was a hopeless task, due to the fraying of the string and the fact that I needed three hands – two to hold the ends of the strings, and one to tie them back together.

A car driving by gently stopped, backed up, and came in to the driveway. A lovely woman called out, as she exited the car, "do you need some help?" She had driven by the flags, and the Temple, and the big Buddha, many times, but she said that she had never seen them until today. All she saw was my struggle and she appeared, ready to help, with some twine that she carries in her car – **because one never knows when one will need twine.** A Buddhist practitioner from another tradition, she was astounded to know that there was a Zen temple right on the main road into Worcester, Massachusetts. We tied up the prayer flags, she offered a stick of incense to our big Buddha, and then went on her way.

One of my Zen ancestors, Haku-un Yasutani Roshi, used to say that when we call out to the universe, *bodhisattvas* arise from the cracks of the earth to come to our aid. And so it was this windy day. **The suffering world is full of compassionate beings, ready to help. They come in many forms, and some drive cars and carry twine with them, because one never knows when one will need twine.**

Receiver practice: Notice moments when you feel particularly in need of help – a feeling of desperation or helplessness, of separation and loneliness. **At these moments, open your attention to the feeling of being disconnected from others.** *Breathe quietly with these feelings of separation, making a big field of awareness that includes these painful feelings, as well as other information coming from your senses: light and color, sounds, smells, sensations, and tastes. Call out to the universe for help, and then wait for a response. Whatever happens, whether it's the sudden awareness of a sense perception, a thought, an emotion, or someone reaching out to you, recognize this as the answer to your calling out.*

Giver practice: Pause in the middle of any activity, any situation, and breathe and be still in your body. Open your senses to who and what is around you and near you. Feel that whatever you perceive as the experience of others is also your experience. If there is some suffering present in the situation, notice if something occurs to you to do, and then just do it, with no expectation of reward.

28

RONALD D. SIEGEL, PsyD, chose this quote:

Love Thy Neighbor as Thyself is more than a commandment – it's a law of nature.

A Patient

THEME – *Loving Self & Others: Quieting the Judgments*

Observing wild animals in Africa, a pattern appears in species after species. Dominant males are surrounded by harems of attractive females. Nearby, young males develop their strength and skills hoping to dethrone the king while young females prepare themselves to join the harem. "Rank" in the troop pretty much determines whose DNA will be propagated.

We may be the "smart monkeys," but our concerns are a lot like those of these other mammals. It's no accident that kids in middle school (who are perhaps closest to our simian ancestors) refer to their insults as "ranking" on one another. As adults, we're a bit more subtle, but concerns for how we compare to others still rule our lives.

Even casual observation reveals that our minds are judgment machines, constantly giving ourselves and others report cards, making comparisons. For example, do you ever find yourself evaluating who is better liked, earns more money, has the nicer car or home, is more attractive, has the more desirable partner or family, is healthier, smarter, or gets more attention or respect? The list goes on and on.

Do you always win in these comparisons? Me neither. And when we lose, our feelings of envy or inadequacy hurt.

Because our self-critical judgments stem from the same hardwired instincts that impel us to judge others, when this system gets going, everyone loses. When our minds criticize others, it's just a matter of time until we become the target of similar self-criticism. **But if we can find a way to accept others, we automatically receive the gift of self-acceptance. In the end, we find that we can only love others to the degree that we can love ourselves, and we can only love ourselves to the degree that we can love others.**

COMPASSION PRACTICE

Letting go of Comparisons

First reflect on recent moments when your mind made comparisons between yourself and others. Note the qualities or criteria that caught your attention (such as wealth, strength, intelligence, attractiveness, generosity, caring, etc.).

Now reflect on why these qualities are important to you. Where did you learn that they mattered? When did you first start using them as criteria to evaluate yourself or others?

*Finally, imagine what your life would be like if you could fully accept yourself and others, regardless of how they "ranked" according to these criteria. Let yourself try to live with the awareness that **judgments don't actually matter.***

29

STAN TATKIN, PsyD, MFT, chose this quote:

"

Compassion automatically invites you to relate with people because you no longer regard people as a drain on your energy.

"

Chögyam Trungpa

THEME – *Compassion for More Loving Relationships*

Buddhist meditation master Chögyam Trungpa (1939-1987) spells out a benefit of compassion that I think also provides an important clue about how to cultivate it. **He refers to compassion as an energized state in which we naturally draw closer to others.** In psychological terms, we might say our ability to be compassionate is inextricably tied to our perceived sense of security – both within ourselves and in our relationships. Conversely, underlying insecurities can make it more difficult to feel compassion and give freely to others.

I suggest we begin by paying attention simply to how we feel around others. How comfortable are we? How easily do we feel drained or fatigued? How secure are we within ourselves?

When I work with couples in therapy, we ask these questions in the context of each partner's relationship style. While some individuals are fundamentally secure, others remain distant from their partner or harbor ambivalence. During our work, partners build their ability to keep each other secure and safe so they can readily repair any hurts, soothe as well as energize each other, and generally love more fully. In the process, they learn to give without fear and to stop seeing the other as a drain on their energy.

What you may not realize is that your security and happiness depend to a large extent on your capacity to focus more on what you can give others than on what they can give you. When you are in touch with your compassion as a giver – and that includes the ability to give compassion and to take care of yourself – you naturally feel energized around others.

Taking to heart the Rinpoche's words, you can move toward a more compassionate stance. Yes, compassion will invite you into more loving and fruitful relationships, but why wait for that invitation when you can take the first step right now?

COMPASSION PRACTICE

You can practice the following whenever you spend time around another person.

1. *Notice your comfort level: are you relaxed or tense, energized or drained? Don't try to change your feeling; just notice it.*

2. *Now consciously shift into the role of giver. This can be subtle – you don't have to say anything or give anything away – just view yourself as a giver. If you were already in that role, fine; just confirm it to yourself.*

3. *As you stay in the giver role, notice how you feel and act. Notice your energy level. Notice the state of your heart. Notice how the other person relates to you.*

As you do this practice over time, see if you detect an increase in your sense of security, in your closeness with others, in your capacity for compassion.

30

JOHN BRIERE, PhD, chose this quote:

We are so lightly here.

Leonard Cohen and Sharon Robinson, **Boogie Street,** *2001*

THEME – *Compassion for Our Fellow Travelers*

It has taken over 15,000,000,000 years for you to appear at this exact moment in time, since the Big Bang first created the conditions that eventually led to who and what you are. Billions of years have ground through the nearly infinite permutations of space, matter, genetics, relatives, and circumstance to bring you and me to this specific point, only to release us in a flash as those conditions inevitably change.

Although we are completely unimportant in this calculus, time is relative and our moment really matters to us. So what can we do? I don't know, but **I imagine the best thing is to celebrate this minute and to care for our fellow travelers.** We are so lightly here, but here we are, intertwined in inevitable circumstance, all of us in this together, either embracing or rejecting the transient nature of life, neither of which really matters in the broader scheme of things.

Time is implacable. It doesn't care, so we must. Love and compassion for others are the only things that make any sense. Winning doesn't, acquiring things is silly in this metric, and vengeance is, at best, ironic when both parties are scheduled to end at almost the same micro-moment in time, with no one really keeping track in any conventional sense. Plus, anger and aggression generally make us (and others) feel bad, which seems like a waste of precious time.

Compassion includes the realization that we are all that any of us have – our appreciation of the spark that we share, the sweetness of our concerns, hopes, preoccupations, and plans, our furrowed brows and happy smiles. Presidents and the homeless, prostitutes and executives, victors and victims, "good" people and "bad" – we are all to be cherished in this brief moment that we have together. What else is there to do?

COMPASSION PRACTICE

A guided meditation

*Take a moment, follow your breath,
do whatever you do to enter a contemplative state.
Let your mind go, let it expand outward, leaving your body,
moving into the sky, then beyond the sky, drifting into
space, past stars, planets, nebulae, and galaxies.
Let yourself float out on the edge of space for a while,
absorbing the grand majesty of the physical universe
slowly wheeling around you in silence. Feel its totality.*

*Then, slowly, return from where you've been,
gliding back through interstellar space, eventually
returning to our corner of the universe. Watch from a
distance as the earth spins on its axis and
orbits the sun, a blue orb set against black velvet
and sharp white lights. Isn't it beautiful?*

*Zoom in further, suddenly aware of the
billions of people of the earth, seeing them
as if through a powerful telescope. See the multitude
of different ages, sizes, races, ethnicities, cultures,
nationalities, and languages. Watch all these people
as they laugh and cry, fight wars and make peace,
give birth and join their deathbeds, doing well
and doing ill, building things and tearing things
apart, but mostly, finally, wanting to connect
with other people, with loved ones, partners,
children, parents, friends. Gather in the sight
of the estimated seven billion human beings
now inhabiting this planet. Feel their plans,
their hopes, their need for happiness and security.
Feel your love for all these people, your wish
that they be content, that they not hurt each
other or themselves, that they live as they
want to live, and that they find peace.*

31

"

True compassion does not come from wanting to help out those less fortunate than ourselves, but from realizing our kinship with all beings.

"

Pema Chödrön

THEME – *Widening the Circle of Compassion*

Nearly all of us live with an unrecognized circle drawn around us. It's a circle of compassion. Those beings inside the circle with us receive compassion because there is little distinction between them and us. When my daughter stubbed her toe on the leg of a table the other day, I immediately felt a tightening of my muscles all throughout my body. I grimaced. My shoulders compressed. I didn't *try* to empathize with her – it was just my natural reaction. If she is sick or hurt, my natural reaction is to help her. She's in my circle.

Some people have a very small circle. They're alone and everyone else is outside. For others, their circle includes their immediate family and may include extended family. There are circles defined by the members of one's church congregation or military unit. The mafia has its own circle. So does a professional football team. Your dog that you've had since he was a puppy may be in your circle. Your neighbor's dog probably isn't.

Most of us involved in spiritual practice think of ourselves as relatively compassionate. But how wide is our circle and how are we disbursing compassion? What would we see if we reviewed our compassion statement the way we review our bank statement?

There are two things we can do. We can work to widen our circle and we can practice with the hope of ultimately dissolving the circle altogether. Widening the circle involves developing a greater sense of kinship with more and more beings. We can develop this perspective through meditation, *Naikan* reflection, and meditative practices like *tonglen*. That is the inside/out approach. The outside/in approach is to engage more with the world, to get to know people more deeply, to understand the nature of their suffering and their lives, to support them and act compassionately towards them.

The narrowness of our circle gives us a sense of separateness, a sense that true, heartfelt compassion is available only for a select few. Einstein referred to this sense of separateness as a delusion, a prison, and called on us to break free and find our kinship with all living beings.

Widening the Circle

1. *Draw a circle on a sheet of blank paper. Inside the circle write the names of some of the people that are already in your circle of compassion.*

2. *On that same paper write the names of a few people you know that are outside that circle. It can include people from whom you are estranged.*

3. *Pick one person from inside your circle and reflect on your relationship with them. Allow an idea of something you can do for them or something you can give them to naturally arise. Act on that idea within 24 hours.*

4. *On a different day, pick one person from outside your circle. Meditate on that person for 15 minutes using the following questions:*

a. *What challenges is he or she facing at this point in time?*

b. *What losses has he or she experienced in the past?*

c. *What is one example of support or help you have received from this person in the past?*

d. *What have you done to contribute to this person's suffering (include ways you tried to help that may have caused discomfort or frustration for them)?*

5. *At the end of your period of reflection, contemplate possible acts of support and compassion that you may be able to offer this person. Ask yourself, If this person were in my circle of compassion, what would I do?"*

Compassion
& the Body

32

KRISTIN NEFF, PhD, chose this quote:

> **My goal isn't to be thin.
> My goal is for my body to be
> the weight it can hold – to be strong
> and healthy and fit, to be itself.
> My goal is to learn to embrace
> this body and to be grateful
> every day for what it has given me.**

Oprah Winfrey

THEME – *Compassion for Our Body:*
"Being Healthy – That Always Looks Good"

Self-compassion is essential to help us through the epic struggle to accept our bodies. **We often tear ourselves to shreds with self-criticism when we don't look the way we think we're supposed to – especially women.** We stare at the super-thin, aerobicized models on the covers of magazines and, not surprisingly, don't feel we measure up. Even the cover girls don't feel they measure up, since most images are digitally enhanced. Given the value placed on beauty in our society, it's not surprising that perceived attractiveness is one of the most important areas in which women invest their sense of self-worth. This is a problem, given research indicating that four out of five American women are dissatisfied with the way they look and that over half are on a diet at any one time. Almost 50% of all girls between first and third grade say they want to be thinner and, by age 18, fully 80% of girls report that they have dieted at some point in their life.

How can we end the suffering caused by our endless criticism of our bodies? By opening our hearts and stopping the internal war. With self-compassion, we don't need to be perfect in order to feel good about ourselves. We can drop the obsessive fixation with being thin enough or pretty enough and accept ourselves as we are; even revel in who we are. **Being comfortable in our own skin allows us to focus on what's really important: being healthy – and that always looks good.**

COMPASSION PRACTICE – BODY SCAN

Body-Acceptance Meditation

This exercise takes about 25 minutes. It's a variation of the meditation commonly known as "the body scan." It's best to lie down on a bed or the floor in what's known as the "corpse pose" in yoga. First, place your hands on your heart as a reminder to be kind to yourself. Feel the warmth of your hands and take three deep, relaxing breaths. Then place your arms by your side again.

Slowly and systematically scan your attention throughout your body. You can go in any order you choose, but a common order is as follows: Start by becoming aware of your right foot, then move your awareness up to your right calf, right thigh, then over to your left foot, left calf, left thigh, to your buttocks, lower back, upper back, pelvic area, stomach, chest, right shoulder, right upper arm, right lower arm, right hand, left shoulder, left upper arm, left lower arm, left hand, neck, face, back of head, top of head.

*As you scan, try to bring a sense of gratitude and appreciation
to the particular body part you're noticing. For instance,
being thankful to your feet for allowing you to walk,
your hands for allowing you to pet your dog, your stomach
for digesting your food, your neck for holding up your head, etc.*

*While you're scanning also notice if any negative judgments
are coming up around that body part, for instance that
your thighs are too big, arms too weak, stomach too flabby, etc.
Whenever these judgments arise, give yourself compassion
for the difficulty of being an imperfect human. Everyone has
aspects of their body they're unhappy with; it is part of the
shared human experience. Try to be kind, supportive,
and understanding towards yourself as you confront the
suffering caused by our continual dissatisfaction with our bodies.*

*The main idea of this meditation is that as you become
aware of each body part, you cultivate both appreciation for how it
helps you and also compassion for any negative judgments about it.*

*When you have scanned your entire body, put your hands
on your heart again and expand your awareness to your
whole body, giving it a shower of affection and gratitude.
Then hold your entire body in compassionate awareness.
Can you – just for this moment – accept yourself and
your body exactly as you are? Love yourself exactly as you are?*

Then gently open your eyes.

33

M. KATHLEEN LUSTYK, PhD, chose this quote:

❝

Every time you smile at someone, it is an action of love, a gift to that person, a beautiful thing.

❞

Mother Teresa

THEME – *A Compassionate Smile*

While we may be very open to giving this gift to others, we can be most reticent to smile upon ourselves.

Over the course of my research career I've done many studies investigating stress and health in women. I've been struck by the amount of self-deprecation and body loathing I've witnessed especially during times of stress and sadness.

Interestingly, the act of smiling engages neural processes responsible for the positive emotions associated with smiling. I've taught women a mindful self-compassion exercise that builds on this scientific principle. The exercise is a body scan that incorporates smiling with each body focal point. While my work is with women, this exercise can easily be done by both genders.

COMPASSION PRACTICE

Lie on the floor with your feet flat on the floor and your knees bent. You may wish to use a yoga strap tied at the knees to relieve the muscles in the legs and any tension in the lower back. Begin with a few moments of breath awareness. Next, follow the breath, as in a body scan, to the feet. As you breathe into your feet, smile at your feet. Feel happiness and gratitude for your feet. Some may be critical of their feet. Perhaps they wish they were smaller or that their toes differed in appearance. Let go of those judgmental thoughts and smile at the amazing creation of your feet. Acknowledge with gratitude the work your feet do for you. As you exhale, let any negative thoughts about your feet leave your body at the point the feet touch the floor.

Continue this exercise moving up the legs, to the hips and buttocks, trunk, torso, etc. With each body part you scan, smile at that body part. Make it a loving smile. Make it a smile you would give someone you care about. Make it a gift of gratitude for the amazing creation of your body. The body is our home for living. We experience our world through our bodies. As we smile upon ourselves, we can cultivate love, appreciation, and compassion for our bodies and ourselves. As Mother Teresa said, such a gift is a beautiful thing.

34

BILL MORGAN, PsyD, chose this quote:

❝

We can never understand
the nature of the mind through
intense effort but only by
relaxing, just as breaking a
wild horse requires that one
approach it gently and treat it
kindly rather than running
after it and trying to use force.

❞

Kalu Rinpoche

THEME – *Compassion Involves Relaxation*

In the old days relaxation was considered to be unimportant in meditation practice, since it allegedly had nothing to do with the freedom we were seeking in the practice of meditation. Plop down and pay attention was the basic format for practice. **Now I see relaxation as central and fundamental, the ground for both compassion and insight. How can compassion arise in a tense body and constricted breath?**

Though we understand this conceptually, seldom does relaxation get the attention it deserves in meditation practice. We are so tense in this culture. Relaxing at the beginning of a meditation session is in itself a profound act of self-care. So too does self-compassion require the relaxing of the breath, mind, and body.

COMPASSION PRACTICE

Compassionate Relaxation in Three Parts:

1. Shaking It Loose

Helping the body to relax is step one. There are a number of ways to do this. These days there is more exposure to yoga, tai chi, qigong. It doesn't have to be fancy. Jack LaLanne jumping jacks are still available. I used to watch Romper Room when I was 4 or 5, and I still remember joining in this exercise:

> *Bend and stretch,*
> *Reach for the stars,*
> *Here comes Jupiter,*
> *There goes Mars.*

That works for me as well as any of the imported approaches. Pretending you are an animal, getting down on the floor and crawling around for a couple of minutes and making the appropriate animal sounds, can also do the trick. Shake out the arms and legs. Do a few neck rolls. The form doesn't matter. What does matter is getting the body a bit more loose and pliable. If you can add a playful dimension right at the start, that's an added bonus.

2. Taking Your Seat

I am not an advocate of straight-as-a-board posture. Nothing else in nature is that straight. You want to be reasonably upright, but also at ease. As you are settling into your posture, try raising and lowering the shoulders, making fists for a few seconds, or opening the mouth wide for a moment or two. These are places where tension is commonly carried. I often scrunch up my face for a few seconds, which brings a childlike sensibility into the moment, just before closing the eyes.

3. Settling the Breath

Now close the eyes, and imagine letting the weight of the body settle more deeply, giving in to the downward pull of gravity.

Take two or three deeper than usual breaths. As you exhale, imagine that the tension and stress are leaving the body, knots of tension melting as the energy moves down through you.

Allow the breath to establish a smooth, easy rhythm as the body continues to relax and the energy moves down and down, as if you were safely secured in a diving bell which was lowering you beneath the waves, beneath the turbulent thoughts and feelings on the surface of the mind, to a quieter and deeper place.

You are watching over this settling process in a kindly, caring way, keeping the breath soft. You can look up at the surface and see the thoughts and feelings up above, but they do not disturb you.

As you become more relaxed, you may begin to notice a pleasant, contented feeling begin to arise. Slowly this feeling begins to spread, to radiate throughout the body and mind, and you are watching over this. Enjoy it.

Now, letting go of the imagery, remain sitting and breathing in this atmosphere of comfort and ease.

■

Feel free to explore your own imagery. I have found the downward flow of energy to be particularly effective in evoking relaxation.

■

Watching over the process keeps the mind engaged in a mindful posture. You don't want to get lost in the imagery or in drifting; knowing what is happening as it is happening is a hallmark of mindfulness.

■

The purpose of visualizing is to evoke a particular affect – in this case relaxation and ease. As the affect becomes stable you can gradually let go of the "training wheels" of imagery

Quotes № 35 to 39

Important Aspects of Compassion

35

PAUL GILBERT, PhD, chose this quote:

##

If at first you don't succeed – skydiving is not for you.

(after Henny Youngman)

THEME – *Compassionate Balance: Perseverance & Limitations*

This, of course, is an amusing little saying but actually it's very important for all of us. It really is about learning to match our goals and expectations to our abilities. There is quite a lot of evidence now that modern society overstimulates our expectations and that we are often disappointed in ourselves and in our achievements because we keep comparing ourselves to other people who do better. We are constantly told that we need to stretch ourselves, test ourselves, and challenge ourselves, but never to sit on our laurels or be content. This has some wisdom to it but, like everything else, it can get out of balance and then becomes a serious problem.

Learning to live within one's own plane of existence can be one of the most important sources of well-being. In Buddhism, craving and grasping are seen as the roots of much of our unhappiness. Now, one of the great sources of craving and grasping is seeing the successes of others and rather than feeling joy for them, feeling inferior and, maybe, envious. This is fueled by a media that tells us that we could and should be doing better. Remember this story?: "If at first you don't succeed, try and try again!" **Perseverance is good but not to the point that we fail to recognize our limitations.** There is a wonderful observation made by someone (I don't recall by whom) that America encourages everybody to see themselves as having equal opportunities. It is said that anyone can become president of the United States. In the last 10 years, given the size of the population, the success rate has not been that high.

There is quite a lot of evidence that some individuals can enjoy activities for the pleasure they bring in and of themselves, but other individuals aren't able to enjoy things for their own sake. Instead, they derive what are called secondary pleasures from them. Either way, **the striving and achieving is focused on social comparison and how they think others see them. For them, life is always a competition and it's not what you achieve particularly, it's what you achieve in relationship to other people.** Imagine that you get a 10% raise at work and you are very pleased with it, but then you hear that the person in the next office got a 20% raise! Tricky, isn't it, the way our pleasures can be simply destroyed by our comparisons? It's no one's fault – it's that tricky brain – but we need to deal with it. Sometimes we just get caught up in striving and striving and hardly have time for actually living.

COMPASSION PRACTICE

Sit comfortably in a chair with an upright back and gently slow your breath to about five or six breaths per minute, breathing slightly deeper and slightly slower than you would normally. After a while you may feel your body feeling slightly heavier in your chair. Think of yourself as becoming grounded, sitting like a mountain, solid and stable. Sense the process of slowing down. As you slow the breath sense the idea of stillness within. This is not relaxation in the sense of having floppy muscles, but a slowing and stilling with an alertness to it.

Focus on the things with which you are happy right now. Notice, perhaps, that you can see the colors of the world and hear the sounds of the world. These are free and do not have to be reached or grasped for. Focus on anything that you can appreciate that gives you pleasure – this could be the first cup of tea of the day (if you're English). In fact, the smaller the pleasures the better because it is learning to pay attention to the small pleasures of life that helps us become content with where we are. As we do this, we begin to learn to enjoy things for themselves and not because they represent some conquest or betterment over somebody else or because they are going to make you look good. Try to spend 5 to 10 minutes every day just deliberately doing something purely for the enjoyment of doing it, with no judgment as to whether you do it well or badly. Savor the actual activity. Pay attention to every aspect of the activity you're doing in this present moment. What fun! There is no need to skydive.

36

RICHARD FIELDS, PhD, chose this quote:

❝

When you plant lettuce, if it does not grow well, you don't blame the lettuce. You look into the reasons it is not doing well. It may need fertilizer, or more water, or less sun. You never blame the lettuce. Yet if we have problems with our friends or our family, we blame the other person. But if we know how to take care of them, they will grow well, like lettuce. Blaming has no positive effect at all, nor does trying to persuade using reason and arguments... No blame, no reasoning, no argument, just understanding. If you understand, and you show that you understand, you can love, and the situation will change.

❞

Thich Nhat Hanh, Peace Is Every Step, *1991, p. 78*

THEME – *Listening without Judgment*

This quote clearly drives home the benefits of compassion and understanding and the negative impact of judging, lecturing, and directing. Listening without judgment, with attention, attunement, empathy, and sensitivity is preferred to persuading using reason and arguments.

For example, a number of years ago, a young man, Brian, was referred to me for counseling by his parents. His parents were concerned that their son had dropped out of college to pursue a career as a member of a band.

I met with Brian individually for only one session and was impressed with his good looks, his affable but quiet personality, and his intelligence and overall smarts. He explained that the band was on the verge of signing a record deal, but it fell through at the last minute. He had not dropped out of school, but decided not to go back after the semester was over. He explained that he needed to spend all of his time and energy pursuing a new record contract and felt he had to put in 120% effort, without the distraction of schoolwork. He was young, 25 years old, and felt he had time for college.

Unfortunately, I had heard this story all too frequently without any positive outcomes, and made the judgment that he was wasting his time. I recommended that perhaps Brian take one course to just keep himself connected with college, a suggestion which he rejected outright.

A few years later I was in my counseling office and took a quick look at a new magazine that was just delivered. On the front cover of *Time* magazine there was a full-page picture of Brian and his fellow band members. I am so glad he never followed my advice.

COMPASSION PRACTICE

When you sense that someone close to you might be ready,
just sit with them; maybe ask a few questions about
what might be going on in their life. Listen to them with
understanding and compassion, no judgment,
no problem solving, no reasoning – just acceptance.

Try this with family, friends, even new acquaintances,
and see an improvement in compassion.

37

EMILIANA SIMON-THOMAS, PhD, chose this quote:

66

Only to the extent that we expose ourselves over and over to annihilation can that which is indestructible be found in us.

99

Karlfried Graf Dürckheim, The Way of Transformation, *1988*

THEME – *Compassionate Courage & Vulnerability*

I encountered this quote when young and broken hearted, and it has stuck with me. This quote by the psychotherapist and Zen Master Dürckheim, cited by Pema Chödrön in her book *When Things Fall Apart* (1997), highlights the universality and persistence of human suffering (i.e. annihilation) and, paradoxically, the boundless strength and resilience that can emerge from engaging with suffering, both our own and that of others.

To me, this quote is about courage and vulnerability, both qualities that are both essential to compassion, but that are sometimes seen as contradictory. According to typical western thinking, courage trumps vulnerability and arms against suffering. Vulnerable people, then, are weak and more likely to suffer. Science does not support this supposition (e.g. extreme risk-takers and bullies have too much courage), and despite popular media's efforts to depict "perma-happy," all-powerful celebrities, everyone suffers. Compassion, our innately endowed response to suffering, requires the courage to be vulnerable and lies at the heart of what is indestructible in us.

Compassion necessarily involves the courage to "expose ourselves" to suffering without fear or a reflexive desire to escape. Without courage, suffering typically leads to distress, anxiety, stoic quashing of feelings or apathetic exasperation. Compassion also requires vulnerability, that is a willingness to openly feel unpleasantness both when bad things happen to ourselves and when they happen to other people. Harnessing the courage to face, to not avoid, suffering – without worrying about what has happened or what could happen next – takes practice.

The last insight I gather from Dürckheim's quote is about the strength, the "indestructibility," gained from welcoming the company of suffering and extending compassion, both towards the self and others. A growing scientific literature is showing that compassion – approaching suffering with loving kindness and a desire to help – is associated with poignant, measureable benefits to health, well-being, and interpersonal functioning.

COMPASSION PRACTICE

The practice that I find most helpful in moments of suffering is to notice sensations as they arise and dissipate and to kindly elect not to get swept away by threat-perpetuating narratives about myself or others, and, importantly, to release the urge to suppress my feelings. Instead, offer a gentle, emotionally authentic, non-judgmental presence. Politely dismiss worried thinking about potential threats or inconveniences. In moments of interpersonal conflict (perhaps those of the greatest suffering), I practice "exchange." I try to put myself into the mind of the other person and look back at my own hurting self. I try to see how I (from their eyes) have made me feel, and how I (the hurting one) am making them feel. This exercise quickly breaks down the sense of "me" vs. "them." This practice joins courage and vulnerability and dissipates hostile suspicious feelings. Nobody is right. Nobody is wrong. There is just now and just us, indestructible.

38

POURIA MONTAZERI, MA, chose this quote:

The gift you offer another person is just your being.

Ram Dass

THEME – *Compassion: A Way of Being*

As these words echo in the four chambers of my heart and its perfume ascends to inform my mind, I am humbly reminded that the sensitivity and the essence of compassion are always here within me. **Compassion is not something one does or achieves. It's not a *doing*, even though we are fixated by its myriad of external manifestations, it's actually a way of *being*. How can *being* be improved?**

When referring to his famous sculpture *David*, Michelangelo said, "I saw an angel in the block of marble and I just chiseled 'til I set him free." I too set out to chisel away the illusion of separateness that permeates my small self (my ego). On the path of rediscovering my essence, ever present under the rubble of misidentifications, self-compassion reveals itself through the heart – a remembrance of what is always present within. This self-compassion then becomes the anchor, the vantage point from which compassion for others can arise effortlessly, for I will no longer see the other as a stranger. I realize that everybody suffers and aches the way I do. I find compassion in this shared craziness. Compassion no longer is an action I am doing to another as if it is mine to begin with. Rather, it is a gift from my being to another being. In Eckhart Tolle's words, "Compassion is the awareness of a deep bond between yourself and all creatures."

COMPASSION PRACTICE

So this week, the gift I offer you is to commit a few minutes of your day to enquire within about compassion. Throw away all the definitions, ideas, and even quotes you have ever heard about compassion. With curiosity and intention, set out to find what compassion really is to you and how you experience it. All fingers point to the moon. Set out to find the ever-present moon within you.

For example, in order for a GPS to be able to lead us step by step towards the address we want to get to through its connection with the satellite, it first needs to know where we are. Accordingly, for you and I, the most important aspect of the journey is to start where we are. So, before doing anything more, rediscover compassion for yourself in THIS moment; a moment that has never happened before.

*In moments that you notice a compassionate feeling
arising for yourself or another, pause, take a deep
breath or two, feel the soles of your feet touching the
ground, and bring your attention to your heart center.
Slow down and simply witness this feeling arising.
Bring your attention to your body. Give some time
and allow this to reveal itself to you naturally.
It is already happening. All you have to do is witness it
and feel it and allow it to inform you. Then notice
the associated thoughts, memories, stories, images,
people, etc., that accompany this process.*

*Through this uncoupling of felt senses and
associated thoughts, you can come closer to the true
taste of compassion that is arising in you naturally.*

*In moments that you witness the development
of compassion in you towards others, notice when
it is effortful and when it is effortless. Be present with
the arising, the action, and the aftermath. Ask yourself
what and who has been fulfilled through this act.*

As the 13th-century Persian poet Rumi wrote:

*Don't ask what love can make or do!
Look at the colors of the world.
The river water moving in all rivers at once.*

39

RICHARD FIELDS, PhD, chose this quote:

66

God grant me the serenity to accept the things I cannot change,

The courage to change the things I can,

And the wisdom to know the difference.

99

Alcoholics Anonymous, Serenity Prayer

THEME – *The Serenity Prayer: Compassion, Surrender, Acceptance, & Limitations*

Having worked in the alcohol/drug recovery field for over thirty-five years, I am well aware that the Serenity Prayer has been recited at the end of every Alcoholics Anonymous, Al-Anon, and Narcotics Anonymous meeting for decades.

The prayer reminds us of the benefits of letting go and surrendering to not only the disease of alcoholism/drug addiction, but also to people and situations that are out of our control. Various Buddhist teachings *(dharma)* describe healthy change as "mindful surrender." Even Superman and Superwoman stayed away from kryptonite.

In a world that promotes, even expects, limitless success and that bestows accolades and constant affirmations one can easily avoid recognizing the value of seeing our limitations. The serenity prayer reminds us to see the value in surrender, seeing our limits, choosing our conflicts wisely, and recognizing the long-term benefits of acting with compassion instead of reaction.

Mark Epstein, author of *Going to Pieces Without Falling Apart* (1999), reminds us of the role surrender plays in opening up to growth experiences: "Buddhism recognizes that the central issues of our lives, from falling in love to facing death, require an ability to surrender that often eludes us."

In our relationships, the struggles and conflicts ultimately come down to our ability to be compassionate towards our own suffering and the suffering of others, as we are reminded in this adaptation of the serenity prayer:

> Grant me the serenity to accept the people I cannot change,
> Courage to change the one I can,
> And the wisdom to know it's me.
> *Anonymous*

So today, and tomorrow, members will keep on coming back to their self-help meetings, and the group will interlock arms, and they will end each and every meeting with the recitation of the Serenity Prayer.

COMPASSION PRACTICE

Choose an important relationship in your life, and practice compassion, tolerance, patience, and acceptance toward that person. Avoid controlling, arguing, criticizing, or attempting to change them.

Recognize and affirm your own powerlessness, while accepting the limitations of the relationship, practicing compassion, and unconditional acceptance.

Notice how this relationship blossoms as you accept, nourish, and support the other compassionately.

Compassion, Hate, & Difficult People

40

RICHARD C. SCHWARTZ, PhD, chose this quote:

I imagine one of the reasons
people cling to their hates so
stubbornly is because they sense,
once hate is gone, they will be
forced to deal with pain.

James Baldwin

THEME – *Hate Blocks Compassion*

Compassion requires that you open your heart to the suffering of others. But what if opening that door to your heart means having to re-experience the pain from your past that you locked away when you closed that door? **Many people keep their hearts closed with hate, judgment, greed, paranoia – all the emotions that block compassion** – because they so fear being overwhelmed by their own hurt if they were to care about someone else's. Instead, they have contempt for their own vulnerability, their sensitivity, empathy, and their neediness. They blame those qualities for getting them hurt in the first place and vow to never again be so weak.

If you cannot afford to care about the parts of you that are suffering, then it's hard to care about people who suffer in similar ways. **If you hate your vulnerability, you will have contempt for those who show theirs.**

When this is true, compassion-building practices alone will not make a lasting difference. **People need to heal their inner pain so that opening their hearts is not so threatening.** They need to compassionately witness what happened to them in the past so as to unload the burdens that make them harden their hearts. Short of that, whatever compassion they feel will be forced and short-lived.

COMPASSION PRACTICE

Spend some time considering all the different reactions you have regarding vulnerability in yourself or in someone else.

When you start to feel sad, hurt, weak, needy, or ashamed, how do you react? That is, are you critical of yourself for feeling that way? Do you distract yourself from that state as soon as possible? Do you hide that vulnerability from others or feel shame if you show it?

When you see someone acting hurt, weak, needy, or ashamed, how do you feel toward them? Is there a part of you that is contemptuous of them, that is glad you're not them and comes up with reasons why you wouldn't be like them? Do you feel uncomfortable in the presence of their vulnerability and try to get away from them as soon as possible?

*The point of this exercise is not to bring you more shame as you become aware of the substantial obstacles to the release of your natural compassion. The point is to provide a starting point for transforming these obstacles. **Approach with curiosity and compassion these protective parts of you that keep your heart closed to your pain and the pain of others. If you can witness and heal the suffering parts, you won't have to work so hard to be a compassionate person. You will just be one.***

41

POLLY YOUNG-EISENDRATH, PhD, chose this quote:

"

In this world
Hate never yet dispelled hate.
Only love dispels hate.
This is the law,
Ancient and inexhaustible.

"

The Buddha, The Dhammapada:
The Sayings of the Buddha, *Thomas Byrom, trans., 1976*

THEME – *Compassion Dispels Hate*

These lines from the *Dhammapada* have always inspired me to remember the core teachings of life: **that only compassion and friendliness allow us to achieve a peaceful way of being.** They are the attitudes that permit us to know ourselves and to know others, especially those whose opinions, views, and ways of life are antagonistic to our own (frequently, these are the people that we live with and are "supposed to love"). The Buddha's words do not imply that we cannot be angry or disagree with one another, but only that **the passion of hatred cannot be dispelled by more hatred.**

When I was a child of twelve, I recall standing in front of a utility sink in the basement of my parents' home and watching a fleeting thought/feeling in my mind's eye: "I hate my father!" This was a kind of awakening. I had not understood why his presence brought me such distress. For example, when he returned to our house at the end of his long workday at the rubber factory, he brought a profound disturbance into the calm and peaceful and clean environment my mother and I preserved. Exhausted and dirty, he stepped through the door and usually my mother shouted out, "Wipe your feet before you come into the kitchen!" That initiated a line of ragged and raw verbal assaults between them that I can now, decades later, see as their inability to allow any love in the presence of their feelings of intrusion and annoyance about one another. They were very different people, my mother and my father. Each wanted to remake the other in her or his image. But it seemed that my father "brought" this disturbance into the house because it wasn't there until he arrived. And so, when I was a child, I sided with my mother.

I didn't realize I was feeling her feelings that day at the utility sink. I thought they were my own. I felt a deep relief to know that this was the character of "hatred." I had never before felt it for anyone else in my life. On only one occasion did I express my hatred to my father ("I hate you! You are ruining our lives!" I said when I was eighteen and he refused to get up from the bed, where my mother had been waiting on him day and night, because he thought he was dying of prostate cancer even though the doctor had told him many times that he had an enlarged prostate, but not cancer). I felt satisfaction in saying it.

Over the many years of digesting my hatred for my father, I came to realize that it was made of "love disappointed" and that my hatred could not have existed without the love. The love was fundamental. I had experienced my father preventing me from feeling the tremendous love that I had felt for him in my youngest years when we were very close. After my mother died, when I was in my fifties (my father having been dead for a couple of years already), I began to feel a deep compassion for my father and to recognize how unfair my mother had been to him.

That compassion released my feelings of love for my father. I have come to regard compassion and love as different experiences although they are related. Compassion opens our hearts as we "suffer with" another. We can open our hearts to strangers – people and animals – whose suffering we witness. I believe that compassion is a natural condition in the human heart because of our original attachment to a mother/other on whom we depend for our own lives. Even a newborn infant can gaze at the face of her mother and attempt to soothe or help the mother. Premature twins who are removed from their mother's womb have been seen to stroke one another's arms to comfort each other.

Love, as distinct from compassion, means that we can deeply accept another, not wanting to change a hair on the other's head. We see the other just as he or she is and we accept all of the agitation, hatred, difference, and inconvenience the other has caused us because the love is bigger than its opposite. Compassion can be the conduit to feeling love in the presence of hatred.

COMPASSION PRACTICE

Metta *Practice*

There are many forms of metta *practice; the one I like best is composed of the following phrases, beginning with my self:*

May I be happy.
May I be free from inner and outer harm.
May I find peace.
May I find ease in living.

I say each phrase aloud at the end of my sitting practice and after I recite a translation of the Metta Sutta. *After stating each phrase, I spend some moments in silence allowing the phrase to soak in.*

After saying the metta *for myself, I repeat the same phrases for my "friends and family." The next round I say for "my enemies and adversaries" and that is where I find my richest insight into compassion. When I think about those people with whom I disagree politically and emotionally, I can see how much they would be helped by happiness, freedom from harm, inner peace and ease in living. I imagine them coming into more warmth and expansiveness and in this way, I can see them as suffering humans just like myself, formulating their opinions and ideals from the ground of their being, just like I do. I imagine all of us relaxing and laughing together – having a picnic. Then finally, I say* metta *for all beings, while holding in mind this warm view of those people with whom I disagree.*

42

SARINA SATURN, PhD, chose this quote:

"

If we learn to open our hearts, anyone, including the people who drive us crazy, can be our teacher.

"

Pema Chödrön

THEME – *Transformative Compassion for Difficult People: "Hurt People Hurt People"*

It is easy to open our hearts to those who have showered us with love, affection, and support. Conversely, it can be quite difficult to open our hearts to those who have caused us aggravation, sadness, and pain. We are emotional creatures and evolutionarily designed to pay attention to and remember the people who bring us well-being, as well as those who cause us harm. Thus, it is natural to adhere to the bearers of goodness and avoid the deliverers of badness. However, it is important for us to recognize our shared humanity. Everyone has struggles, triumphs, hopes, and fears.

The most intolerable people we encounter can turn out to be our greatest teachers. How can this be? **They can teach us about ourselves: buttons to push, areas of sensitivity, and patterns of insecurity.** They can also teach us about others: the ways in which judgment, ignorance, lack of exposure, and acting out of negative emotions can cause injury. This brings to mind the old adage that proclaims, **"Hurt people hurt people." Indeed, people who lash out and wound others are often times experiencing deep anguish themselves.**

To grow compassion within ourselves, it is essential to plant the seed of understanding so that we may grow to love everyone, including those who seem very unlovable at times. These difficult people may need our love most of all. When we begin to understand where others are coming from, and how they came to be the way they are, **we will come closer to finding peace within ourselves by finding liberation from the shackles of resentment and remorse. It is transformative to cultivate a compassionate, forgiving, open, and loving heart for all people, including cherished ones, objectionable ones, and ourselves.**

COMPASSION PRACTICE

Sit down in a quiet place, place your hands over your heart, and practice mindful breathing for several inhales and exhales.

First, bring to mind a person whom you love deeply. Think of a very tender moment you have shared with this individual and feel the affection flow through your body. Reflect on the warm feeling this recollection brings to you. Then, think of a difficult moment that occurred with this person – perhaps an argument, misunderstanding, or hurt feelings – and think about how you moved through this conflict and still hold this person very dear despite this bump in the road. Think of how this person has taught you about your capacity for compassion and love. Now turn back to the caring moment you shared and allow the gratitude and kindness to wash over you:

May you experience abundant compassion.
May you find forgiveness for yourself and others.
May you discover gratitude for the lessons taught to you by others.
May your pains and sorrows soften.
May you feel our shared humanity.
May you find peace and love in your heart.

*Next, think of someone who drives you crazy. This may be
a relative, co-worker, friend, acquaintance, or a stranger who did
something to really bother you. Reflect on what this person may have
experienced in order to act in ways that hurt you. Perhaps his or her
upbringing, genes, stressors, environment, and/or suffering caused
this person to rub you the wrong way. Realize that this person is
also one of your greatest teachers:*

May you experience abundant compassion.
May you find forgiveness for yourself and others.
May you discover gratitude for the lessons taught to you by others.
May your pains and sorrows soften.
May you feel our shared humanity.
May you find peace and love in your heart.

*Finally, turn to yourself. Reflect on all your great qualities,
including your capacity to love and forgive. Realize that you too have
hurt others in the past and that we are all human. Move back to
holding yourself in the light with self-compassion. Radiate good
wishes for everyone in this world, including yourself:*

May I experience abundant compassion.
May I find forgiveness for myself and others.
May I discover gratitude for the lessons taught to me by others.
May my pains and sorrows soften.
May I feel our shared humanity.
May I find peace and love in my heart.

Quotes № 43 to 52

Compassion for Difficult & Challenging Situations

43

FRANK OSTASESKI chose this quote:

> **How far you go in life depends on your being tender with the young, compassionate with the aged, sympathetic with the striving and tolerant of the weak and strong. Because someday in life you will have been all of these.**

George Washington Carver

THEME – *Turning Toward Suffering*

Compassion arises as an intelligent and appropriate response from our being in the presence of suffering. There is no shortage of human suffering in our world so it is reasonable to ask if compassion arises as a response to suffering and there is so much suffering, why isn't there more compassion? Perhaps it is because we so rarely allow ourselves to actually face and touch the suffering directly. We are masters of distraction.

Healing is always found by going toward suffering. A common misunderstanding of compassion is that you should help someone feel safe; to help him or her feel there is no danger. This is fine of course, if you can do it, but in my hospice work I have seen that for many, dying does not feel safe. However, **when I am compassionately present, the patient begins to trust and be open not because there is no danger, but because they sense an attunement, felt as support, which enables them to go toward the suffering**.

Compassion expresses the gentleness, the kindness necessary for our heart and our soul to relax and to trust. Without the presence of compassion we cannot fully open to suffering. Often the presence of compassion heals a particular pain right away. But sometimes the presence of compassion allows us to stay with what might otherwise be too difficult to tolerate. By staying with the experience of suffering, compassion allows a deeper truth to be revealed.

It seems that the real significance of compassion is not exactly about removing suffering, it is about cultivating our capacity to be with suffering. This increased tolerance for suffering allows us to set down our defenses. When our defenses are down we can look objectively to see the actual causes of suffering. Then we can act skillfully to help remove those causes.

COMPASSION PRACTICE

Consider each of the following questions:
1. *What is a way that you try to avoid suffering?*
2. *How do you experience compassion?*

*Use journaling, contemplation, or open-ended inquiry
to discover what is true. Sense the body, feel the heart
observe the mind. Track and report what is occurring
as it occurs. Release yourself from the habit of knowing
or the pressure of censorship. Simply respond to
the questions spontaneously, truthfully, and compassionately
from a place of curiosity. It can be helpful to repeat
the questions to notice how your responses change. Let yourself
experience the impact of your answers.*

44

DONALD MEICHENBAUM, PhD, chose this quote:

"

Opportunities to find deep powers within ourselves come when life seems most challenging.

"

Joseph Campbell

THEME – *Resiliency & Compassion: "Post Traumatic Growth"*

When really bad things (traumatic events) happen to good people, such as the experience of natural disasters, serious accidents, life-threatening illnesses, and exposure to violence – such as terrorist attacks, combat, and sexual victimization – people are usually impacted in the immediate aftermath. However, most individuals (some 75%) evidence resilience, or the ability to bounce back from, adapt to, and overcome such ongoing adversities. In fact, some individuals, families and communities evidence **"post-traumatic growth."** It is not as if these individuals do not also at times experience strong emotional reactions, since post-traumatic distress and resilience can co-exist. **Joseph Campbell's quote reminds us that challenges can bring out our best qualities.**

In contrast, some 25% of victimized individuals will evidence ongoing distress, adjustment difficulties and, in some instances, persistent psychiatric disorders such as Post Traumatic Stress Disorder (PTSD), depression, anxiety, and alcohol/drug abuse and dependence.

Among the many things that distinguish these two groups of 75% versus the 25% are the nature of the "stories" that they tell themselves and that they share with others. Resilient individuals are able to view themselves as moving from being "victims," to being "survivors," and even "thrivers."

Resilient individuals are able to be more compassionate toward themselves and toward others. Compassion, as well as other positive emotions like optimism, gratitude, perseverance/grit, and forgiveness can facilitate the recovery process.

COMPASSION PRACTICE

Envision a good friend or favorite relative who is in the same situation as you. He or she has come to you for help. Think about ways you could listen non-judgmentally and WITH COMPASSION.

What would you say?
What would you do?

Could you use the same understanding, kindness, warmth, and support toward yourself that you would offer your friend or relative?

Can you introduce your "Compassionate Self" to your "Suffering Self"?

Think about ways to move forward without self-blaming, self-criticizing, and stress-engendered behaviors.

You are in charge of your rate of progress, your journey to resilience and personal growth.

Can you begin to "restory" your life?

45

CHRISTINE A. COURTOIS, PhD, ABPP, chose this quote:

66

So how do you sit with a shattered soul? Gently, with gracious and deep respect. Patiently, for time stands still for the shattered, and the momentum of healing will be slow at first. With the tender strength that comes from an openness to your own deepest wounding, and to your own deepest healing. Firmly, never wavering in the utmost conviction that evil is powerful, but there is a good that is more powerful still. Stay connected to that Goodness with all your being, however it manifests itself to you. Acquaint yourself with the shadows that lie deep within you. And then, open yourself, all that is you, to the Light. Give freely. Take in abundantly. Find your safety, your refuge, and go there as you need. Hear what you can, and be honest about the rest: be honest at all cost. Words won't always come; sometimes there are no words in the face of such tragic evil. But in your willingness to be with them, they will hear you; from soul to soul they will hear that for which there are no words.

99

Kathy Steele, "Sitting With the Shattered Soul," Pilgrimage: Journal of Psychotherapy and Personal Exploration, *1989, 15 (6), p. 24*

THEME – *Compassion for the Shattered Soul (Trauma)*

I chose this quote because I have been taken with it for many years and often use it at the end of treatment workshops. I also included it at the end of my book *Healing the Incest Wound* (2010). Kathy Steele is a friend who has long inspired me in my work with trauma survivors. She models her philosophy and her quote captures her compassion and the spiritual dimension and respect needed to work with the traumatized.

The lesson is to sit quietly, join the person, be patient, and listen. Witness and be present and attuned in order to break through what is often the excruciating isolation and wordless silence of the trauma survivor. Your presence will communicate respect and compassion, even when there are no words. This is especially important when the trauma is interpersonal and has created a chasm of mistrust between self and others. Mindful presence is, in and of itself, healing.

COMPASSION PRACTICE

*Sit quietly in a centered way, using your breath to quiet you.
Once you are calm, focus on what it means to have a shattered soul.
Allow yourself to resonate and empathize with those who
have been shattered. Open your heart and mind to the
suffering involved. Send your energy and kindness and
know that you do not need words to be with them.*

*Gently end the practice when you are ready and let yourself
know you can make a difference by witnessing and by caring.*

46

"

All beings want to be happy, yet so very few know how. It is out of ignorance that any of us cause suffering for ourselves or for others.

"

Sharon Salzberg, Lovingkindness:
The Revolutionary Art of Happiness, *1995, p. 78*

THEME – *Happiness & Compassion in Lieu of Unhappiness (Dissatisfaction) & Shame*

In our striving for happiness we fuel our fear of unhappiness and, in so doing, we lose sight of happiness and joy in our present, moment to moment life.

We often see joy and happiness as something we will attain in the future. We delude ourselves in thinking that when we have enough money, the right job, the right relationship, the right car and house, the right family situation, then we will be happy. In striving for these things we can lose sight of the happiness and joy available to us in the present moment. We forget to breathe and live life, and enjoy each moment, each breath. The Dalai Lama says it well: **"If you want others to be happy, practice compassion. If you want yourself to be happy, practice compassion."**

COMPASSION PRACTICE

When you are in what I call a "grumpy" mode with feelings of discouragement, frustration, and dissatisfaction, it is hard to have gratitude or even acknowledge the good things in your life. Anger and fear have replaced happiness and compassion, especially compassion for oneself.

You can shorten your time in "grumpy" mode by not personalizing situations, reducing expectations of others, letting go of feelings of inadequacy and shame, disputing distorted realities, and accepting all feelings, including dissatisfaction.

You can stop suffering and begin to feel compassion for yourself. You can be more present, enjoying life more and being more compassionate towards yourself and others.

List those things, people, and situations that bring you happiness.

You might then send a letter of gratitude and appreciation to those people in your life who help bring joy, happiness, goodness, contentment, and security to your life.

47

GINA ARONS, PsyD, chose this quote:

> **"**
>
> And now here is my secret, a very simple secret; it is only with the heart that one can see rightly, what is essential is invisible to the eye.
>
> **"**

Antoine de Saint-Exupéry, The Little Prince, *1943*

Our capacity for compassion is strongly linked to our ability to listen to the voice of the heart. Most days there is much on our minds that distracts us from what really matters. How easy it is to be pulled by feelings of inadequacy, competition, greed, anxiety, sorrow, or depression – any of which can distract us from the loving, understanding voice of the heart.

In my work as part of a collaborative law team helping couples through divorce, I encourage people to understand their lives and those around them through a lens of compassion. The divorce process may seem a strange place to look for compassion. And yet, compassion is perhaps most needed where it's least likely to arise spontaneously.

At the end of a relationship there is usually so much pain, sorrow, and disappointment. It is much easier to focus on injustice and the faults of the other. When this pain silences the voice of the heart, more hurt and suffering arises. Sometimes people are afraid to look beneath the surface and listen to what the heart can see because there is a fear it will lead to unbearable pain. Still, allowing our hearts to guide us can lead to the most balanced and respectful agreements. By exploring what is truly important to each person and working to help both people feel safe, heard, and understood, people heal, move on, and are able to remain in each other's lives in a new way.

Compassion for ourselves and for others offers us a path to understanding and seeing the world more clearly. We remember "what is essential is invisible to the eye." We wonder what lies beneath the surface, tolerate ambiguity, and engage in questions and conversations that can lead to new perspectives.

COMPASSION PRACTICE

Notice the negative moment and practice seeing what is "invisible to the eye."

See if you can notice a moment when you judge yourself. Allow yourself to hear the harsh judgment.

Pause.

Focus on what is "invisible to the eye." Speak to yourself with a voice of understanding from the heart. Speak in a tone that you would use with a person you love and respect deeply. Notice how you feel when you treat yourself with love and compassion.

Next try this in an interaction with another person. Choose a moment when someone does something that annoys or hurts you. If you are like most of us the first reaction is to think, "What's wrong with that person?" Notice any temptation to make negative assumptions.

Instead, ask the other person what they're experiencing: "What just happened?" Allow yourself to be open to other explanations. You may be surprised by the answers.

May the moments of noticing the negative give you a window into what is "invisible to the eye" and allow you to see with your heart and act with compassion.

48

RICHARD FIELDS, PhD, chose this quote:

66
Addiction:
Land of the Hungry Ghosts
99

Buddhist Cosmology

THEME – *Compassion for Alcohol/Drug Relapse*

Buddhist cosmology describes addiction as the "Land of the Hungry Ghosts," where people have huge appetites that are unable to be quenched or satisfied. Buddhism describes addiction as a "false refuge," a delusional place to try and hide and escape from being present in life with the good and the bad. Addiction is viewed as the inability to see the goodness in ourselves and in others.

Three major reasons that people relapse are:
- **negative emotional states (reactivity)**
- **abstinence-violation effect**
- **shame (disconnection)**

Self-compassion can help to reduce reactivity and overcome the shame of relapse.

Self-compassion for violating abstinence is reframed as information that strengthens recovery, that supports recovery (i.e. recovery-prone versus relapse-prone behaviors and situations), and strengthens one's support system instead of shaming, isolating, and disconnecting oneself. The Alcoholics Anonymous proverb that "silence is the enemy of recovery" reminds one to seek support and to talk about urges, cravings, and relapse. Relapse is not viewed as a failure, but as a natural event and as an opportunity to connect (not isolate) and to be gentle with oneself, rather than shaming or blaming oneself.

COMPASSION PRACTICE

"Urge Surfing"

Ironically, disregarding the urge or craving to relapse, whatever it is, will do more harm if ignored or denied. It is common to have negative or unhealthy urges or cravings. This might come in the form of dreams, interactions, being in the wrong place at the wrong time, and/or being vulnerable to HALTS (Hungry, Angry, Lonely, Tired, Sick).

"Urge surfing" is a mindfulness relapse-prevention practice that can help put cravings and urges in a natural cycle that can be tolerated and understood, without reacting (i.e. using alcohol/drugs). Alan Marlatt, PhD, and his colleagues at the University of Washington used "urge surfing" as a technique in their Mindfulness Based Relapse Prevention (MBRP) program.

Whatever the urge or craving, you can use "urge surfing" to get through it. Visualize the urge or craving as an ocean wave. The wave has a beginning, a crest, and a smooth cycle until it crashes on shore and then rolls to conclusion. The wave visualization helps one realize that we can tolerate the urge, and breathe through it and its associated desires. It reminds us that we can delay reaction and that urges will quiet with focus and time.

Try "urge surfing" this week and notice how it works and what arises and emerges.

49

DENNIS TIRCH, PhD, chose this quote:

❝

The essence of human bravery is refusing to give up on anyone or anything.

❞

Chögyam Trungpa Rinpoche,
Shambhala: The Sacred Path of the Warrior, *1984*

THEME – *Courage & Compassion*

How is it that compassion involves courage? Why should loving kindness embolden us to overcome anxiety? As it turns out, activation of our compassionate mind involves powerful regions of our emotional brain, known as the **attachment system. This system stems from our evolved human caregiver capacity and it provides us with the ability to face difficult feelings and danger.**

Research has established that when we experience compassion and empowering affiliative emotions, we down-regulate the activation of the threat detection system in the brain, effectively evoking the courage we need. In this way, compassion allows us to be brave, to turn towards suffering, and to overcome the conditions that can make our lives smaller and more painful.

In Buddhist art, we can find images of the pure white lotus, symbol of compassion and purity, blossoming from out of the mud. Similarly, compassion emerges from the depths of painful experiences and dark emotions.

Compassion is about touching the pain of existence, even when it brings us face to face with dark feelings and impulses. Just like the lotus, our compassion arises when we get into the mud and face the essential pain in our nature.

Our compassionate courage, the essence of our bravery, accepts all of who we are, as individuals, and as members of our species. With compassion, we are opening our hearts in loving kindness to the entire human family. Recognizing that all beings wish to be happy, to be well, and to flourish, our compassionate minds dwell in a place of sensitivity and action to alleviate suffering, rather than in a space of contemplation and condemnation. We give up on no one, least of all ourselves. We extend compassionate wisdom, compassionate intention, and compassionate action, again and again. **Just as water gradually smoothes away jagged rocks, our compassion gradually brings the courage and peacefulness we need to heal our anxious suffering.**

Compassion Flowing Out

Begin by simply following the breath in and out of the body,
aware of your physical presence, just as it is, in this very moment.
Allow the breath to find its own rhythm and pace.
Whenever attention wanders, gently draw your attention
back to this moment, by focusing on the breath.

After a few minutes, bring your attention to a memory of a time
when you felt compassionate towards another person.
This can be a time when they were in need of a helping hand.
You can even bring your attention instead towards the compassion
you felt for an animal or pet. Remember a time of relative peace.
Remember the sensory details of being in the presence of a
person for whom you felt great warmth, loving kindness, and support.

As you imagine feeling kindness and compassion towards another,
see if you can imagine yourself expanding as the warmth
and care of your intention grows. As you inhale,
imagine yourself drawing compassion into you through the breath.
As you exhale, feel compassion flowing out of you towards this loved one.

With your attention on the flow of your breath, observe your desire
for this person to be happy, for them to be filled with compassion,
for them to be peaceful and at ease, and for them to be well.

Imagine your compassion touching their heart.
Imagine that the burden of their suffering is lifted
little by little with every breath. Sense again the compassion flowing
out of you, and joy and peace flowing into the person with whom
you are sharing kindness. With your next natural exhale,
let go of this representation of the other person and draw your attention
simply to the experience of compassion in yourself.
Recognize where in the body your open and heartfelt desire
to share kindness and helpfulness presents itself.
Allow yourself to rest in this feeling of loving kindness for others,
feeling the presence of compassion for others as it flows through you.

When you feel you are ready, exhale and let go of this exercise, giving yourself
some credit for having had the courage to engage in this practice.

50

STAN TATKIN, PsyD, MFT, chose this quote:

"
To ease another's heartache is to forget one's own.
"

Abraham Lincoln

THEME – *Compassionate Service*

At the root of compassion is the ability to feel empathy and to place others' needs before one's own. We may not think of looking to Abraham Lincoln for spiritual guidance, yet a careful study of his battle with suicidal depression reveals a deeply spiritual soul with tremendous capacity for empathy and loving kindness. In fact, Lincoln survived his major depression in part through **his belief in service to others**. He rose above his personal woes and allowed himself to stand for a cause that was greater – the alleviation of the suffering of others.

As a couples therapist, I see many partners suffer alone needlessly, oftentimes viewing each other's pain as an indictment of their own inadequacies. A huge portion of my effort as a therapist is to help partners learn to care well for one another and to remind them that they are each responsible for providing the other with speedy relief from heartache, fear, threat, or insecurity. **This service partners provide to one another is based on true mutuality, compassion, respect, gratitude, and loving kindness.** It is given not because it is deserved, routinely returned, or expected; rather, it is given because compassion is what connects us both to others and to our own inner selves. It is how we defeat our own suffering. It is also how we guarantee the long-term survival of a relationship. As Lincoln also famously said, "Kindness is the only service that will stand the storm of life and not wash out."

One might wonder if offering kindness to ease another's heartache is sufficient. In other words, why forget one's own heartache? In my work, I have seen that the kindling of compassion is made difficult by over-focus on the self. Preoccupation with our own suffering makes it hard to even perceive the value of compassion. We become so caught up in the fear that our needs will not be met that we can't see beyond that. A vicious cycle is created whereby self-centeredness precludes us from offering compassion, which in turn isolates us and prevents us from opening to true mutuality.

This cycle is only broken when it is replaced by a reverse cycle. Merely trying to forget our own heartache is unlikely to work; self-centeredness is not an easy a habit to break. However, we can make the effort through regular practice to engage in acts of kindness. We can soothe a partner, listen to a friend's woes, and offer a helping hand. The irony is that in so doing, our own heartache is naturally and effortlessly diminished and ultimately quieted.

The Latin root of compassion is com + pati ("to suffer with"); patience also derives from pati (to suffer). **Patience is an important aspect of compassion because it buffers the tendency to be self-centered.** *You can practice patience and compassion whenever you are with a partner, family member, or friend in distress by following these steps:*

1. Invite the person to say whatever is on his or her mind.

2. As you listen, instead of focusing on your reactions or offering your opinion, consciously breathe in patience and breathe out compassion.

3. Feel patience filling your body as you inhale. Picture loving compassion enveloping the other person as you exhale.

4. If the person is too distressed to talk, you may do the same practice as you sit together in silence or as you hold him or her.

As you experiment with this practice, it may be tempting to focus on how it affects the other person. However, my suggestion is to notice instead whether it expands your ability to respond with compassion.

51

ROSHI MARSHA LINEHAN, PhD, chose this quote:

"

It is not enough
to be compassionate.
You must act.

"

His Holiness the Dalai Lama, 2008

THEME – *Compassionate Action: Helping Others to Get Out of Hell*

The Oxford English Dictionary gives several definitions of compassion. "Suffering together with another," and "the feeling or emotion, when a person is moved by the suffering or distress of another, and by the desire to relieve it," are two such definitions. Both definitions leave out the actual act of doing something to relieve the suffering of the other.

When you are the one suffering, compassion alone is simply not enough. Georges Bernanos, a French novelist and political writer, said, "I know the compassion of others is a relief at first. I don't despise it. But it can't quench pain, it slips through your soul as though a sieve." This sums up my thoughts exactly. *Wanting to help another is simply not sufficient.* **Finding ways to do it, learning what we need to know to relieve the suffering of others, developing the skills to be effective – these are what matter at the end of the day.**

When I was a supervisor, I once rebuked a supervisee for reinforcing a client's sense of her own helplessness. The therapist had felt the distress of her client to such a degree that she almost immediately reached out and swept away the event causing the client so much pain. After the rebuke, it was clear my student thought I had no compassion.

So I told her the following story: "Imagine a person is standing in hell, standing on coals on fire, jumping up and down and screaming, 'Help, help, bring me some water and pour it on my feet! I can't stand this. I am burning up.'" Then I asked her who she thought was most compassionate – the person who runs to get a pitcher of water and climbs down into hell to pour the water on the poor soul's feet, or the person who rushes down to hell, gets behind the poor soul and pushes, saying, "Let's get out of here."

Her answer was remarkable. "Marsha," she said, "the difference between us is that you think you can get people out of hell." Her response was very important because if it were true that she could not help get people out of hell, then she was correct – pouring water would be the wise thing to do.

A year or so later, the therapist called me to thank me. She had learned skills that allowed her to give up on clients less easily in the service of teaching them how to get out of hell.

This story illustrates my passion for evidence-based treatments. It is all too easy to provide a compassionate ear to those in hell. We feel better ourselves and, at times, listening brings temporary relief to the other person. It is undoubtedly better than no relief and occasionally it may really be all that we can offer. But what if we took the time to learn more effective ways to help? What if we learned the evidence-based treatments that are out there for the learning? What if we insisted that others learn them, not to avoid suffering one client's pain with them, but to add actions that are known to help? Would not that be the more compassionate response?

The compassion practices that go with this story are two-fold.

First, *when listening to others in pain, it is important to be mindful of not only the other person's suffering, but also of our own.*

Mindfulness of current emotions and sensations is important because through it we learn that indeed we can tolerate both our suffering and that of others. Breathe in and notice sensations of emotion. Breathe out and notice sensations of emotion. Noticing, allowing, in and out.

Second *is the practice of "wise mind." Remind yourself that each of us has the capacity for universal wisdom. Though it may be difficult to reach, it is possible. Breathe in deeply, let your mind drop to your center; listen to the silence within, listen in the depth of the emptiness that is itself wisdom. Breathing in and out normally, letting yourself settle into wisdom itself, asking, and, at times, questioning; listening for an answer (but not answering). Breathing in, breathing out, dropping into the silence.*

52

SYLVIA BOORSTEIN, PhD, LCSW, chose this quote:

"

May all beings, omitting none, feel safe and content and happy, and live with ease.

"

The Metta Sutta

THEME – *The Metta Sutta: A Compassionate Wish for the Well-Being of All*

It has been my experience from the start of my career as a psychologist that therapists practicing across the spectrum of therapies agree that the essential healing element in all therapeutic collaborations is the sense of being truly seen. I believe that even more healing than the sense of being seen is the conviction that someone wants to see us and is willing to suspend preconceived ideas, views, and opinions in order to do that.

Seeing people as people just like myself, without preconditioned stories, allows me to remember that everyone suffers and delights, just as I do, in this ever-challenging life and evokes in me empathic responses of compassion or joy that do not depend on particulars. I would like to be able to wish, as the *Metta Sutta* instructs, "May all beings, omitting none, feel safe, and content, and happy, and live with ease." To the extent that I can "see" others on this intimate level, I will feel supported by my own natural benevolence.

We haven't as a species, gotten there yet, but maybe we will. **We are wired, I believe for compassion, so I am hopeful that we can achieve that connection.**

COMPASSION PRACTICE

*This last compassion practice reminds us
to practice the* Metta Sutta's *theme of compassion for all beings:*

*May all beings, omitting none, feel safe, and content,
and happy, and live with ease.*

Appendix

Contributors

Photo Credits

Contributors

Richard Fields, PhD, Editor *QUOTES NO. 11, 36, 39, 46, 48*
Richard is the founder/director of FACES Conferences (www.facesconferences.com), the mission of which is to bring mindfulness and compassion training to mental health professionals.

He has over thirty-five years experience specializing in outpatient alcohol/drug relapse prevention and recovery. He is the author of the college textbook, *Drugs in Perspective*, 8th ed. (2012).

He is also the author of *Awakening to Mindfulness* (2008) and is the editor and contributing author of the book *A Year of Living Mindfully: 52 Quotes & Weekly Mindfulness Practices* (2012).

Gina Arons, PsyD *QUOTE NO. 47*
Gina is a clinical psychologist with over 25 years of experience. She is a Collaborative Law coach and a mediator. She maintains a private practice in Lincoln, MA and serves on the board of the Massachusetts Collaborative Law Council.

Roshi Melissa Myozen Blacker, MA *QUOTE NO. 27*
Melissa is a Zen priest and resident teacher at Boundless Way Temple in Worcester, Massachusetts, and Abbot of Boundless Way Zen. She is the coeditor of *The Book of Mu* (2011) and does private spiritual direction and mindfulness consulting (www.melissablacker.com).

Sylvia Boorstein, PhD, LCSW *QUOTE NO. 52*
Sylvia is cofounding teacher of Spirit Rock Meditation Center. She is the author of five books on Buddhism, mindfulness, and meditation. She is the author of *Happiness Is An Inside Job: Practicing for a Joyful Life* (2008).

Tara Brach, PhD *QUOTE NO. 6*
Tara is founder and senior teacher of the Insight Meditation Community of Washington, DC and teaches Buddhist meditation at centers in the United States and Canada. A clinical psychologist, she is the author of *Radical Acceptance* (2003) and *True Refuge* (2012) (www.tarabrach.com).

John Briere, PhD *QUOTE NO. 30*
John is Associate Professor of Psychiatry and Psychology at USC and Director of the Psychological Trauma Program at LAC+USC Medical Center. He is the recipient of the APA Award for Outstanding Contributions to the Science of Trauma Psychology (www.johnbriere.com).

C. Daryl Cameron, PhD *QUOTE NO. 9*
Daryl is Assistant Professor of Social Psychology at the Univ. of Iowa. His research focuses on the causes and consequences of compassion. He has also examined how regulating compassion can create its own costs by changing moral identity and moral principles.

Christine A. Courtois, PhD, ABPP *QUOTE NO. 45*
Christine is a Board Certified Counseling Psychologist in independent practice in Washington, DC. She is the author of *Treatment of Complex Trauma: A Sequenced, Relationship-Based Approach* (2013) and is the co-founder as well as Clinical and Training director for The Center: Posttraumatic Disorders Program, Washington, DC.

Brooke Dodson-Lavelle, MA *QUOTE NO. 4*
Brooke is a Doctoral Candidate at Emory University. She has helped develop and adapt Cognitively-Based Compassion Training (CBCT) for schoolchildren as well as adolescents. She served as the associate-training director of the CBCT Teacher Training Program, which she co-developed.

Christopher Germer, PhD *QUOTE NO. 2, 17*
Chris is a Clinical Instructor in Psychology at Harvard Medical School. He is the author of *The Mindful Path to Self-Compassion* (2009) and coeditor of *Wisdom and Compassion in Psychotherapy* (2012), and *Mindfulness and Psychotherapy*, 2nd ed. (2013).

Paul Gilbert, PhD *QUOTE NO. 10, 20, 35*
Paul is head of the Mental Health Research Unit as well as Professor of Clinical Psychology at the University of Derby, United Kingdom. He has been developing compassion-focused therapy for people with high shame and self-criticism. He is currently a series book editor for *Compassionate Approaches to Life Difficulties* with New Harbinger (USA) and Constable Robinson (UK).

Elisha Goldstein, PhD *QUOTE NO. 14, 19*
Elisha is a psychologist in private practice in West Los Angeles, CA. He is the author of *The Now Effect* (2012) and the co-designer of the 8-week program CALM - Connecting Adolescents to Learning Mindfulness.

Susan Kaiser Greenland, JD *QUOTE NO. 15*
Susan is the author of *The Mindful Child* (2010) and a former corporate attorney. Susan developed the Inner Kids program for children, teens and their families and teaches worldwide.

Roshi Joan Halifax, PhD *QUOTE NO. 13, 24*
Joan is a Buddhist teacher, anthropologist, author, and social activist. She is the Abbott and head teacher at Upaya Zen Center in Santa Fe, NM. She is the author of many books, including *Being with Dying* (2008).

Jack Kornfield, PhD
QUOTE NO. 1

Jack is an internationally renowned meditation teacher and one of the leaders in introducing Buddhist practice and psychology to the West. Trained as a Buddhist monk in Thailand, Burma, and India, he is the co-founder of Spirit Rock Center in northern California. He is the author of many books including *A Path With Heart* (1993) and *The Wise Heart* (2008).

Gregg Krech
QUOTE NO. 31

Gregg is a leading expert in Japanese Psychology and the Director of the ToDo Institute in Vermont. He is the author of *Naikan: Gratitude, Grace, and the Japanese Art of Self-Reflection* (2002) and *A Natural Approach to Mental Wellness* (2011) (www.todoinstitute.org).

Roshi Marsha Linehan, PhD
QUOTE NO. 51

Marsha is Professor of Psychology, Director of the Behavioral Research & Therapy Clinics, Univ. of Washington, and author of *Cognitive-Behavioral Treatment of Borderline Personality Disorder* (1993).

Allan Lokos
QUOTE NO. 5, 8

Allan is the founder and guiding teacher of The Community Meditation Center in NYC. He is the author of the best seller *Patience: The Art of Peaceful Living* (2012) and *Pocket Peace: Effective Practices for Enlightened Living* (2010).

M. Kathleen Lustyk, PhD
QUOTE NO. 33

Kathy is professor of Psychology at Seattle Pacific University. In addition to teaching Behavioral Neuroscience and Women's Health courses, she is the Primary Investigator of the Lustyk Women's Health Lab (www.spu.edu/LustykLab).

Donald Meichenbaum, PhD
QUOTE NO. 44

Don is a Distinguished Professor Emeritus from the Univ. of Waterloo, Ont., Canada. He is a recipient of a Lifetime Achievement from the American Psychological Assn. He has published extensively and his most recent book is *Roadmap to Resilience* (2012) (www.roadmaptoresilience.org).

Pouria Montazeri, MA
QUOTE NO. 38

Pouria is an innovative transpersonal psychotherapist and educator with a private practice, You be You Counseling, in Boulder and Denver, CO. He teaches at Naropa University's Graduate School of Psychology.

Bill Morgan, PsyD　　　　　　　　　　　*QUOTE NO. 34*
Bill is a founding board member of the Institute for Meditation and Psychotherapy in Boston, MA. Bill teaches residential retreats for mental health professionals, and has recently completed 4 years of intensive retreat.

Kristin Neff, PhD　　　　　　　　*QUOTE NO. 18, 21, 32*
Kristin is a pioneer in the field of self-compassion research and the author of *Self-Compassion* (2011). She is an Associate Professor of Human Development, Culture & Learning Sciences at the Ed. Psych. Dept. of the Univ. of Texas at Austin.

Frank Ostaseski　　　　　　　　　　*QUOTE NO. 43*
Frank is a Buddhist teacher, founder of the Metta Institute, and co-founder of Zen Hospice Project, the first Buddhist hospice in America. He is one of America's leading voices in contemplative care of the dying. Frank can be reached at www.mettainstitute.org.

Jenny Phillips, PhD, MSN　　　　　　*QUOTE NO. 25*
Jenny is the author of *Letters from the Dhamma Brothers: Meditation Behind Bars* (2008) and the producer of the award-winning documentary film *The Dhamma Brothers*. Jenny has a private practice in Concord, MA.

Sharon Salzberg　　　　　　　　　　*QUOTE NO. 16*
Sharon is one of America's leading meditation teachers and writers. Her most recent book, *Real Happiness* (2010), is a New York Times Bestseller. She is also author of *The Kindness Handbook: A Practical Companion* (2008), and *Lovingkindness: The Revolutionary Art of Happiness* (1995).

Sarina Saturn, PhD　　　　　　　　*QUOTE NO. 42*
Sarina is an assistant professor at the School of Psychological Science at Oregon State Univ. She received her PhD in neuroscience from NYU and was a postdoctoral fellow at the Univ. of California, Berkeley, CA. Her current research investigates the biology underlying prosocial emotions.

Richard C. Schwartz, PhD　　　　*QUOTE NO. 3, 7, 40*
Richard is the developer of the Internal Family Systems (IFS) model of psychotherapy and the president of the Center for Self Leadership, which coordinates training programs in IFS around the world (selfleadership.org). He has written 4 books and over 30 articles or chapters on IFS.

Shauna L. Shapiro, PhD　　　　　*QUOTE NO. 23, 26*
Shauna is an Associate Professor of Counseling Psych., Santa Clara Univ., CA, a licensed clinical psychologist, and an expert in the integration of mindfulness into Western Psychology. She coauthored the text *The Art and Science of Mindfulness* (2009).

Ronald D. Siegel, PsyD *QUOTE NO. 28*
Ron is Assistant Clinical Professor of Psychology, Harvard Medical School and serves on the Board of Directors and faculty of the Institute for Meditation and Psychotherapy. He is the author of *The Mindfulness Solution: Everyday Practices for Everyday Problems* (2010) and coeditor of *Mindfulness and Psychotherapy*, 2nd. ed. (2013).

Emiliana Simon-Thomas, PhD *QUOTE NO. 37*
Emiliana is the Science Director at UC Berkeley's Greater Good Science Center. She studies the connection between health and well-being in relation to being grateful, mindful, generous, and kind.

Stan Tatkin, PsyD, MFT *QUOTE NO. 29, 50*
Stan is a clinician, researcher, teacher, and developer of a Psychobiological Approach to Couple Therapy (PACT). He has a clinical practice in Calabasas, CA and is the author of *Wired for Love* (2011).

Dennis Tirch, PhD *QUOTE NO. 49*
Dennis is the founder/director of The Center for Mindfulness & Compassion Focused Therapy. He is the author of *The Compassionate Mind-Guide To Overcoming Anxiety* (2012).

Amy Weintraub, MFA, ERYT-500 *QUOTE NO. 22*
Amy is a pioneer in the field of yoga and mental health for over 20 years. She is the author of the best-selling *Yoga for Depression* (2004) and *Yoga Skills for Therapists* (2012). She is the founder/director of the LifeForce Yoga Healing Institute (www.yogafordepression.com).

Michael Yapko, PhD *QUOTE NO. 12*
Michael is a clinical psychologist living in Fallbrook, CA. He is internationally recognized for his work in clinical applications of hypnosis, treating depression, and developing strategic, outcome-focused psychotherapies. He is the author of *Mindfulness and Hypnosis* (2011), *Trancework*, 4th ed. (2012), and *Depression is Contagious* (2009).

Polly Young-Eisendrath, PhD *QUOTE NO. 41*
Polly is a Jungian analyst and psychologist in private practice in Central Vermont. She is the author of the book *Compassionate Kids in an Age of Self-Importance* (2008).

Photo Credits